Praise for *How To Be Right*:

'I know few broadcasters as consistently, forensically, brilliant as James O'Brien. Here, he shows us – with empathy, edge and exquisite comedy – how it happens.'
– Emily Maitlis

'Intelligent, funny and worrying. An unsurprisingly brilliant read from a great broadcaster. I vehemently wish that everyone would read it. The world and this country would be a better place if they did.'
– Gary Lineker

'A simply brilliant read ... I love this book!'
– Jamie Oliver

'This book is required reading to slice through the rhetoric, slogans and bluster of politics and politicians. James is the broadcaster we need right now, setting the world to rights one call at a time.'
– Susanna Reid

'Funny, wise and passionate. Like Yoda with better grammar.'
– Danny Wallace

'Funny, clever and alarming ... a modern day travelogue through the airwaves with all the mistrust, misinformation, contradictions and manipulation laid bare.'
– Krishnan Guru-Murthy

HOW
TO BE
RIGHT

in a world
gone *wrong*

JAMES O'BRIEN

WH
ALLEN

3 5 7 9 10 8 6 4 2

WH Allen, an imprint of Ebury Publishing,
20 Vauxhall Bridge Road,
London SW1V 2SA

WH Allen is part of the Penguin Random House group of companies
whose addresses can be found at global.penguinrandomhouse.com

Penguin
Random House
UK

First published in the United Kingdom by WH Allen in 2018
This edition published in the United Kingdom by WH Allen in 2019

www.penguin.co.uk

A CIP catalogue record for this book is available
from the British Library

ISBN 9780753553121

Printed and bound in Great Britain by Clays Ltd, Elcograf S.p.A.

Penguin Random House is committed to a sustainable future for
our business, our readers and our planet. This book is made
from Forest Stewardship Council® certified paper.

MIX
Paper from
responsible sources
FSC® C018179
www.fsc.org

For Lucy McDonald, who has taught me, among so many other things, that winning the argument doesn't necessarily mean you were right.

Above all, don't lie to yourself. The man who lies to himself and listens to his own lie comes to a point that he cannot distinguish the truth within him, or around him, and so loses all respect for himself and for others. And, having no respect, he ceases to love.

Fyodor Dostoevsky, *The Brothers Karamazov*

CONTENTS

Introduction   1

Chapter 1: Islam and Islamism   24

Chapter 2: Brexit   51

Chapter 3: LGBT   76

Chapter 4: Political Correctness   102

Chapter 5: Feminism   125

Chapter 6: Nanny States and Classical Liberals   149

Chapter 7: The Age Gap   170

Chapter 8: Trump   190

Epilogue   213

Afterword   221

A Note on the Text   228

Acknowledgements   229

INTRODUCTION

I AM A VERY rare beast. I am a liberal talk show host. And as such, my job is something of a contradiction.

The true liberal is cursed with a desire, even a duty, to understand other points of view. It's a world view that admits disagreement and dissent but seeks to establish objective parameters by which the fundamental truth of things can be judged. The best way to achieve this is to ask the holders of those differing views to explain the reasoning that has led them to their conclusions. As a phone-in radio show presenter, I have probably had more opportunities to hear from ordinary people over the last few years than almost anyone else on the planet, but sadly digging deep into the foundations of a firmly held, but often evidentially flawed, opinion is rarely as simple as it sounds, nor as commonplace as it should be.

In stark contrast to the traditional liberal, the traditional radio talk show host is usually so desperate to win every argument that he – and this particular breed of broadcaster is almost always a he – essentially constructs an echo chamber of epic proportions and invites callers to pay homage at the altar of his ego. They are called 'talk shows' for a reason and monologues have come to play a big part in my work but, when actually interacting with callers, less talking and more listening has, in the second half of the fourteen years I've been doing it, yielded much more satisfying results.

For my own part, I'm happy to employ a little bombast in defence of my own positions (and even happier to explain and justify them properly), but am always keenest to hear people who disagree with me – about everything from immigration to feminism, obesity to Islamist extremism – attempt to explain and justify their own positions. I would love to claim otherwise – you need at least a slightly overdeveloped ego to do the job, after all – but the fact that they rarely manage to do so is not necessarily testament to any particular talents on my part. It is a simple reflection of the fact that hardly anyone is asked to explain their opinions these days; to outline not just *what* they believe, but *why*.

Even more worryingly, the way in which furiously held convictions so often collapse under the scantest scrutiny speaks to a British society which has morphed during my years on air into a space where, for reasons we will explore, people who once felt compelled by common decency (or 'political correctness' as they often prefer to describe it) to keep their most vile views to themselves, now feel free to shout them from the rooftops. Racism is enjoying a resurgence on both sides of the Atlantic on a scale I would have considered impossible just five years ago. The sort of language and ideas once confined to my most ignorant and bigoted callers have found their way into the White House, and the world seems split into people who find this immensely gratifying and people who find it all as puzzling as it is terrifying.

Anti-semitism, weapons-grade misogyny, white supremacism, homophobia and quite horrible attempts to frame all Muslim people as complicit in the actions of any Muslim terrorist or criminal have moved squarely into the mainstream media. I believe that this has happened precisely because divisive sloganeering and rancid rhetoric have gone unchecked. In short, people are not being challenged to justify their views, or to explain *why* they think what they do.

Financial crises and the ensuing hardening of the daily struggle just to get by have always left populations susceptible to the stoking of ancient hatreds, and millions of refugees fleeing wars can quickly be turned into scapegoats for public sector failings by people seeking popularity and power. The job of describing and challenging this process traditionally falls to the liberal, the truth-teller, the objective journalist, but they are a cowed breed right now, all too conscious that comforting lies deliver more clicks, viewers, listeners and profits than uncomfortable truths.

This, I think, is why so many of my own encounters with people utterly persuaded of their own righteousness but, often to their own shock and horror, completely unable to justify any of it, have enjoyed so much success online recently. It has been undeniably good for my career, but somewhat less so for my soul.

Almost everywhere, blatant lies are offered up as 'balance' to demonstrable truths; exaggerations and embellishments are allowed in the interests of 'impartiality' and any attempt to correct misleading statements is decried as evidence of an unspecified but deeply suspect 'agenda'. Why should 'Bob in Sunderland' or 'Julia in Richmond' expect their views on, say, immigration to be challenged when every time they turn on their radios and televisions or open their newspapers they see respected establishment figures expounding similar views unchallenged, unchecked and, it often seems, unceasingly?

So let's begin with immigration.

Contrary to what many people claim, you *can* talk about it in this country without being called a racist. I should know, I've been doing it for over a decade and nobody's ever called me one with a straight face. Indeed, it's hard to imagine quite how the phone-in radio format would survive without the regular deliveries of conversational red meat that immigration issues routinely provide. While being told regularly that it is a taboo topic, there have been times over recent years when it's felt like we talk of little else.

Nevertheless, the notion that you somehow can't talk about it without being called a racist is a perfect example of a hollow, deliberately deceitful slogan or catchphrase moving largely unquestioned into the mainstream of public discourse. The importance of distinguishing between people who tell lies for personal gain and people who believe them for personal reasons will be a recurring theme throughout this book. I'm not sure it's ever more blurred than it is here.

It is almost always the case, when dealing in the rhetoric of hatred and division, that each popular slogan is a cynically finessed evolution of an altogether nastier one. This particular claim is the bastard child of the less familiar refrain that you can't say what you *really think* about immigration without being called a racist. And this, for many people, is of course quite true. Their private beliefs about people from countries or cultures other than their own are demonstrably racist, they just don't like being told so. I'm not sure why, and I suspect the next chapter in these ludicrous, social media-fuelled 'culture wars' will see more and more people take the advice that Donald Trump's former *consigliere*, Steve Bannon, gave to French fascists to wear the accusation of racism with 'pride'[*]. For now, the kindest thing you can do in the circumstances is invite them to say whatever they want with a promise that you won't call them names.

Three or four years after I first assumed the position behind the microphone, I was told by a caller from the London borough of Hounslow that he wasn't allowed to say what he really thought about immigration because of political correctness. I remember it partly because I lived in the same borough

---

[*] Speech to the national assembly of France's National Front, Lille, 10/3/2018.

at the time and partly because what followed provided one of those moments where even the presenter is left spluttering in shock at what has just emerged from the radio.

'Go on. Say what you really think about immigration, John. I promise not to call you a racist or cut you off for being politically incorrect. Just take a deep breath and say it.'

There was a pause, an audible inhalation of breath, and then: 'Alright. Hounslow's full of Pakistanis and they all stink.'

Can you debate with John? Can you let his claim go unchallenged? Should you keep your promise not to call him racist? And can you answer any of these questions without inflating at least a little bit the notion that free speech is being somehow stifled by well-meaning attempts to cleanse the national conversation of naked prejudice?

This is, perhaps, an extreme example, but it is an illustrative one. John is patently wrong – I have personally smelled several British/Pakistani residents of Hounslow and sundry other boroughs – but he believes that for you to tell him so is for you to seek to censor him. When people like him, and there are plenty who employ altogether more sophisticated language and sophistry to make similar points, demand that their right to free speech be respected, what they are really demanding is that their speech be free from scrutiny. John is entitled to make his ludicrous claim but feels that you should not be entitled to call it out for the racist claptrap it so clearly is.

The most important lesson I have learned in this job is that it usually serves no purpose to respond with counter-claims or condemnations. Only by asking John further questions can you get to the heart of him. For example:

> **James:** What do they smell of, John?
>
> **John:** Curry.
>
> **James:** All of them, John?
>
> **John:** Yes.
>
> **James:** Do you like curry, John?

The moments just before he says 'Yes' are the ones you come to work for. There's something in the pause, the catch of breath that, however brief, tells you and almost everybody listening that he does like curry. And that the smell of curry, never mind the smell of people who supposedly all smell of curry, is clearly not the source of his problem with immigration. Or, to be more precise, with immigrants. It is their existence, or at the very least their presence in *his* Hounslow, that offends him.

Oddly, a curious truthfulness often comes into play at times like these, and I haven't managed to work out why that is. Perhaps it's because most people are fundamentally honest, even when ashamed of whatever it is they're being honest about. Or perhaps they're not ashamed at all and only 'lefty do-gooders' like me expect them to be. Or perhaps there's something about the format, the knowledge that (in those days) a couple of hundred thousand people are listening, that compels honesty. Although, of course, it often doesn't and those encounters can be even more illustrative of the mess in which we've all allowed ourselves to become immersed.

I remember a caller from Colchester, let's call him Bob, who pursued the always popular line of accusing me personally of being insulated from the horrific effects of immigration by dint of being middle class and a resident of the leafy London suburb of Chiswick, an area that my dedicated handful of unapologetically – but always anonymous – racist internet trolls laughably describe as a 'white enclave', despite it having over three times more immigrants than the national average.

It is clearly neither racist nor hard to imagine feeling unsettled by women walking in the streets of your home town with their faces covered or shops with frontages in incomprehensible languages. But it is equally not a feeling likely to have been fermented on the mean streets of Colchester, a picturesque market town in Essex. And if Bob's opinions are honest and based on his personal experience, rather than spoon-fed headlines about the people most recently arrived in this country, then he's not going to struggle with my simple questions.

James: Talk me through the realities I'm missing, Bob. How has immigration affected you personally? And I don't mean the fact that your doctor or your milkman or your window cleaner might hail from foreign lands, I mean the negative stuff. The stuff that prompted you to call in.

Bob: The schools are full, the hospitals are full ...

James: Have you ever been turned away from A&E, Bob? Do you know anyone who has?

Bob: Well, no, but that's not the point—

James: Have you personally encountered a single child – and I'm happy to take this at third or even fourth hand – who has been left without a school place at the beginning of the academic year in an area of above average immigration?

Bob: Of course I haven't, but everyone knows class sizes are increasing every year

James: Are you a Conservative voter, Bob?

Bob: Used to be.

James: Did you hear Iain Duncan Smith on the show last week offering up the fact that there are more people in work than ever before as proof that his policies are working?

(This, obviously, refers to a distant time when government ministers agreed to be interviewed on my radio show. In fact, I think that was the very last time one did.)

Bob: Yes.

James: Do you remember when I pointed out that there were more people alive than ever before so this was hardly a reliable measure of progress?

Bob: Yes.

> **James:** You just did the same thing with schools. The fact that there are more kids in school than ever before is neither necessarily good nor bad. It's just counting.

In all honesty, I may have been in danger of losing Bob – and indeed the proverbial room – at this point. So back to the simplest, and most important, question of all. If you didn't end up here through personal experience, how did you?

> **James:** So, in terms of your personal experience of issues related to current immigration levels, what would you say offered up the strongest support for your belief that it's bad? Just one thing that if I lived with you in the Colchester 'hood, instead of in the leafy white enclave of Chiswick, would see the scales falling from my eyes faster than you can say: 'Your home town was literally founded by Romans'.
>
> **Bob:** You can't get to the tills at my local shop.
>
> **James:** Come again?
>
> **Bob:** I cannot get to the tills at the shop.
>
> **James:** Because of all the immigrants?

(A pause. Positively Pinteresque in its proportions.)

> **Bob:** Yes.

I probably should have left it there. But I didn't.

> **James:** Have you ever asked the shopkeeper how he feels about you wanting to deport all his customers?

Do you feel sorry for Bob? Is he racist? I'm not sure. He's clearly a bit of a plank, but we can all be guilty of plankishness. And he has clearly been led far enough down the rabbit hole of racist scaremongering to have lost sight of daylight. But is that his fault? Again, I'm not sure. But if you fast forward a couple of years from that phone-in to the immediate aftermath of the UK's Brexit vote and have a look at the *Sun*, the country's top-selling newspaper, edited by church-going Catholic Tony Gallagher, you'll get a pretty clear idea of how someone like Bob can end up so confused.

On 27 June 2016, the newspaper carried a double-page spread trumpeting: 'Where the Brex Was Won: Streets full of Polish shops, kids not speaking English … but Union Jacks now flying high again.'

Just 24 hours later – and I'm going to use the *Sun*'s own words here to avoid any danger of misrepresentation – 'as cops probed more than 200 hate crimes in the wake of last week's referendum result', Gallagher published this editorial:

The Sun *today calls on Brits of all creeds, colours and race – Leavers and Remainers – to come together for the good of the country. We are appalled at reports of racist abuse in the*

wake of last week's EU vote, and utterly condemn attempts
to provoke division in our society. Anyone caught inciting
racial hatred must feel the full force of the law.

It's the 'utterly condemn attempts to provoke division in our society' that beggars belief. That and the fact that the two pieces of 'journalism' were separated by a single day. It doesn't make me sympathetic to Bob's position, but it does make me sympathetic to a man pushed into such positions by 'journalists' like Gallagher. Also on his watch, columnist and disgraced former editor Kelvin MacKenzie claimed to have proof that Muslims 'are different from the rest of us'*. Another columnist on Gallagher's roster infamously explained how 'pictures of coffins' and 'bodies floating in water' would not make her care about refugees**. I'm often asked how I felt when that particular columnist was briefly employed by the radio station where I work. 'Soiled' comes closest.

Whether it is the immigrant family with an enormous council house or a horribly misguided decision to take the Union Flag down from a council building, these instances are news precisely because they are as rare as hen's teeth. In the hands of an editor like Gallagher, however, they are served up as though commonplace, as proof that 'we' are somehow being overwhelmed by 'them'. It's heady stuff and leads to people like Bob

---

* The *Sun*, 12/4/2016.
** Katie Hopkins, The *Sun*, 17/4/2015.

not even realising that they have developed pungent opinions while possessed of precisely no proof to support them.

It seems to me that there are only two ways in which someone with no experience of immigration negatively impacting his life can be convinced that it is doing so: first, the scaremongering served up daily by editors like Gallagher can warp the strongest mind, and second, a deeply held prejudice against all incomers and resentment of their very presence here ('Curry John' would be a contender). If popping people in the former category is patronising, then so be it. I prefer to see it as a fundamental belief in the basic decency of people despite so much evidence to the contrary.

Taken to its extreme, the results of this scaremongering can be truly tragicomic. Since I started presenting a phone-in show, I've become a lot more interested in understanding how callers like the one I'm about to describe have ended up where they are, than I am in trying to 'dismantle' them. The problem is that you have to strip their arguments right down to the bone to determine where they come from. On a good day, it makes for a riveting listen. On a bad day, it can make you despair. This chap provided a bit of both.

There are a few phrases that set off alarm bells. 'Political correctness gone mad' is obviously one of them, and so is 'eroding British values' and 'multiculturalism is destroying Britain'. Andy in Hemel Hempstead employed all three in the opening two minutes of a call addressing, I think, the question of what we actually mean when we talk of 'British values' and what makes people think they're somehow under threat.

I've never understood this argument. You could stick me in the middle of China and feed me nothing but chlorinated sweet-and-sour chicken and I'd still feel a patriotic swell at the opening bars of Hubert Parry's score for 'Jerusalem'; even more so at the words of the poem Blake wrote. Ditto Shakespeare, Dickens, Thomas Hardy and Kenneth Wolstenholme's commentary of the closing moments of the 1966 World Cup final. I have tried to imagine what people are feeling when they talk of these 'values' disappearing and I can't. Because they're not. We'll look later at how one particular newspaper editor likes to obsess about such 'values' while routinely denigrating Parliamentary sovereignty, the independence of the judiciary and academic freedom, which seem to me among the most valuable of British values, but for now, consider Andy.

James: But how are your values being eroded?

Andy: This isn't a Christian country anymore.

James: Do you go to church, Andy?

Andy: No.

James: What do you mean, then, when you complain about this not being a Christian country? There's nothing stopping you from being a practising Christian, nothing at all. You've elected not to be one.

Andy: We're being overrun by other faiths and cultures and we're bending over backwards to accommodate them.

Again, these phrases and claims are as commonplace as they are unchecked, and if Andy can read variations thereof everywhere from the *Sun* to the *Spectator* why would he ever stop to wonder whether they're true? They're designed to make him angry and fearful, not peaceable and thoughtful.

James: OK. So if you're really worried that Christians are being outnumbered by followers of other faiths, and I have to tell you, mate, that the numbers really aren't on your side here, then there's absolutely nothing to stop you redressing the balance by shipping the whole family to Mass on Sunday.

Andy: That's not the point. We're doing too much to accommodate other cultures and not enough to protect our own.

James: Give me an example.

Andy: Eh?

James: Give me an example of something that makes you feel your own Christian culture, albeit one you're not practising, is being diminished by efforts to accommodate the feelings or faiths of people who aren't part of it.

Andy: OK. We looked around a school for my daughter to go to the other day and it had a prayer room for Muslim students.

James: What's wrong with praying?

Andy: Nothing but it was just for Muslim students. How can that be fair? This is Britain.

Now, for the avoidance of doubt, there may be such policies at schools somewhere in Britain and if there are, they're wrong. Religious segregation is, for me, a line that should never be crossed. Have a prayer or a 'peaceful time' room by all means if you've got the space, but it has to be open to everybody. Come to think of it, I'd call that equality of accessibility a 'British value'. And also, of course, a 'liberal' one.

The point is that I had never heard of it happening before and, truth be told, I didn't believe him. It was too convenient an example, too much of a piece with the catalogue of predictable complaints that had come before.

So I asked him the name of the school and he told me. And I had a quick scoot online and I couldn't find any reference to a 'prayer room' or a particular predominance of Muslim students. And I did something I've never done on air before or since. I lied: 'Andy, we've got the headmistress on the other line and she doesn't know what you're talking about.'

Andy hung up. I don't know why he wanted, perhaps even needed, the narrative of being overwhelmed and under threat to be true. So much so that he made stuff up to prove it. But I know that he embarrassed himself only because he was asked, politely and calmly, to provide some proof of what he claimed and, apparently, believed. Most of the columnists and editors and commentators whose ugly lead he was following are never asked to do the same.

Of course, people can and often do refuse to explain them-selves, insisting that even politely requesting them to do so is a sign of 'political correctness' or 'cultural Marxism' or the result of 'Common Purpose' indoctrination. 'Common Purpose' is a British-funded charity that runs leadership programs around the world but, in the fetid minds of newspaper editors and conspiracy theorists, it is a secretive cabal dedicated to smuggling liberalism and tolerance into British society. You've probably never heard of it but the *Daily Mail* describes it as being 'like some giant octopus, Common Purpose's tentacles appear to reach into every cranny of the inner sanctums of Westminster, Whitehall and academia ...'* In other words, for many of my most profoundly mistaken callers, their truths are self-evident and in need of no defence or explanation whatsoever. These are not bad people, but it is almost impossible to explain how they've ended up in such a mess without portraying them as at best gullible and at worst dangerous.

And these days I never want to do that. Certainly, the radio format lends itself to cajoling and castigation to a degree that can sometimes seem close to bullying. But there is something truly remarkable about a person holding an opinion with such confidence that they call a radio programme with a million listeners, presented by a person with a reputation for scrutinising arguments more closely than most, only to discover that they have no idea why they believe what they profess to believe. And it's this confidence that's key. The call screening process on the programme is relatively straightforward: has this

---

* *Daily Mail*, 16/11/2012

person been on recently? And do they sound as if they really mean what they're saying (as opposed to just fancying a few minutes on the wireless)? It takes about thirty seconds to get, respectively, a no and a yes and the caller will then be placed in a queue to come on. Of course, some of the people who lack the courage or confidence to call in have persuaded themselves that the people who end up embarrassing themselves on air have been specially selected for the weakness of their position. In fact, the opposite is true. There's no point me talking to someone who doesn't sound completely convinced that they're right and I'm wrong. It's the strength of this conviction that I find enduringly fascinating.

Long before Donald Trump deployed the phrase 'fake news' to punt his own barefaced lies while discrediting honest journalism that was critical of him, the British media was breathtakingly complicit in portraying immigration as an unalloyed bad. Pockets of resistance at the *Guardian* and elsewhere were preaching almost pointlessly to the choir, while the likes of Kelvin MacKenzie at the *Sun* and latterly Paul Dacre at the *Daily Mail*, inarguably the two most powerful and toxic propagandists of the last 30 years, were offering up generous portions of xenophobic fire and brimstone on a daily basis.

It wasn't just that immigration *might* be a factor in sundry perceived problems. Immigration was *the* problem.

Take, for example, a few hardy perennials: immigrants undercut our wages, immigrants put a strain on public services and immigrants are responsible for the housing crisis. These are widely held and not particularly racist convictions, but even if you allow that they are partly true, which is not at all clear, immigration can never account for either the existence or the scale of the perceived problems.

To be temporarily trite, substitute the three instances of the word 'immigrants' above for the word 'people' and you will see that exclusively blaming the former for the travails of the latter only helps to excuse the employers who aren't paying decent wages, the politicians who are underfunding the public sector and the property developers who aren't building houses.

Conveniently, some of my own erstwhile colleagues in the media provide a poignant case in point here. When I worked at the once mighty *Daily Express* in the late 1990s it was owned by a Labour Party peer, edited by a founder of the feminist *Spare Rib* magazine and was embarking upon an ambitious attempt to produce popular liberalism as an antidote to the toxic-but-ineffably-popular scaremongering and deceit being perpetrated by its historic rival, the *Mail*.

It was not an entirely successful venture. I inexplicably ended up as showbusiness editor and, in 2000, shortly after I surrendered the post to rescue my liver and have a crack at broadcasting, the paper was sold to a publisher and pornographer. His name was Richard Desmond and his political convictions were so rock solid that his proprietorship saw the paper's support move from Labour to the Conservatives to the right-wing extremists, Ukip.

As it did so, its editors inevitably sought to propagate some of the myths and exaggerations popularised by the *Mail*. Chief among them was the idea that immigration was driving down the wages of 'British' workers. (I put British in quotes here because, for me, anyone working in Britain is a British worker, just as anyone working in a fish and chip shop is a fish and chip shop worker.)

Readers, though dwindling in number, lapped it up; the letters page and, later, online comments section groaned under the weight of feisty defenders of the national interest insisting that we sling out these hard-working wage-deflators pronto, and anyone who questioned the rationale for doing so (like me) would be routinely told that we'd soon change our tune if a Pole offered to come and do our job for a fraction of our fee.

It's heady stuff. All you need to do to prove that Poles (other Eastern Europeans are available but the Poles tend to bear the brunt of this particular brand of baiting) have driven down your wages is a) Be unhappy about how much you get paid and b) Find a Pole doing the same job. In the crucible of tabloid provocation, it's all their fault.

One rather pertinent point was never mentioned by the journalists writing about the issue, or the editors instructing them to do so, or the proprietor throwing the weight of his paper's political support around like a frisbee in the hope, perhaps, of securing a peerage. Namely, that from April 2008 to January 2017, most journalists on the Express Group's four national titles received pay rises of precisely zero pence – not even a consideration to reflect the rise in living costs they would have been reading (and writing) about in their own news pages.

Meanwhile, in 2014 alone the company reported pre-tax profits of £333.7 million. This isn't a conspiracy or an example of political correctness going mad or a refusal to stand up for British values. Rather, it is an incredibly simple, entirely evidence-based example of a newspaper proprietor who sacked staff, enacted swingeing, real-term pay cuts across his entire workforce and trousered epic amounts of moolah for himself (Desmond is estimated to have taken £350 million out of the company during his 17 years of ownership) while enthusiastically telling 'British' workers that their wages were being reduced by immigrants.

The *Daily Mail*, where former editor Paul Dacre's career-long mission to terrorise Middle England with fears of imminent immigrant invasion has prompted many of my younger callers to describe relations with older relatives being profoundly and permanently damaged, provides an even more telling vignette. As recently as March 2018, almost two years after the paper's shameful weaponisation of immigration helped to deliver a Brexit set to make almost everyone poorer, cleaners at the newspaper's Kensington office were being paid, via an outsourcing company, £7.50 an hour, the legal minimum for workers over 25 years of age but considerably less than the 'London Living Wage', a calculation based on what it actually costs to live in the capital. Given that the majority of the 31 staff hailed from the Caribbean, Africa and South America this could, I suppose, have been offered up as evidence of migrant workers driving down wages.

Of course, if Dacre had been minded to portray the people who polish his desk every morning for just north of 15 grand a year as architects of national wage deflation he would have been wise to keep mention of his own annual remuneration – £2.37 million in 2017 alone – off the page.

Even less likely to enjoy any mention in his titles is a campaign undertaken in early 2018 by the United Voices of the World trade union. On behalf of the 31 cleaners, they secured over 100,000 signatures on a petition demanding they be paid the London Living Wage of £10.20 an hour and organised strike action. While the paper's owners insisted that the decision had nothing to do with the UVW's actions, or the petition, or the threatened strike, March 2018 saw the cleaners secure the desired pay rises.

So, a newspaper which routinely peddles the notion that immigration drives down the wages of 'ordinary' workers had its offices cleaned by adults earning about £15,600 a year, while its editor received £2.37 million.

And when collective bargaining, under the auspices of a trade union, appeared to secure precisely the sort of pay rises *Daily Mail* readers are routinely told they are being denied by immigration, the paper's owners passed it all off as a remarkable coincidence. You will, needless to say, struggle to find any mention of this episode in any right-wing British newspaper because right-wing British newspapers despise trade unions, and the complete demonisation of immigrants in the workplace can obviously only work when carried out in tandem with the demonisation of trade unions. Only then can people be successfully persuaded both that their working conditions are undermined by foreigners *and* that joining forces to seek improvement to those working conditions is dangerous, quasi-Communist claptrap.

That it all seems so obvious makes the question of why people embrace these manipulations so enthusiastically all the more perplexing. The only answer I've come up with after years talking with countless Johns and Bobs and Andys is that they somehow enjoy being frightened. And dominant elements of the media stoke those fears because it has always been easier and more lucrative to sell tickets for the ghost train than for the speak-your-weight machine. I'm not expecting any prizes for this insight.

This book will attempt both to help people shrug off the crippling chains of these misinformed fears and furies and also suggest some tactics which friends and family members might employ to help the afflicted to do so.

Chapter 1
ISLAM AND ISLAMISM

IT'S HARD TO BELIEVE now, but growing up with an apostrophe in your surname in Britain in the 1970s and 1980s was often enough to see you accused of supporting the IRA. My late father, who spent most of his career as a journalist on the staunchly pro-Union *Daily Telegraph*, kept a small collection of hate mail from readers accusing him of everything from using his job to surreptitiously spread 'Fenian propaganda' to having the blood of murdered children on his hands. He framed some of the choicest examples and hung them in the downstairs loo at home. These days, with the advent of email, Twitter and Facebook, he could have papered the whole house a hundred times over.

I was never exposed to much more than playground ribbing, but I do remember thinking, even then, that the people who sought to conflate people like me and my dad with the men and women who detonated bombs in two Birmingham pubs in 1974, killing 21 people, were in many ways doing the work of the terrorists for them. The more fractured and divided a society becomes, the more fertile the ground is for terrorists to plant their views and ideologies.

Nevertheless, when the full force of Islamist terrorism was first felt in the West on 11 September 2001, I was stunned by how quickly some people sought to paint all Muslims as somehow complicit in the atrocity. Of all the news-based issues we have subsequently covered on the radio show, this one depresses and confuses me the most. A British Muslim not only knows that she is just as likely to be a victim of attacks on the London Underground or the Manchester Arena as anyone else, but also that she will, before the bodies of the victims are cold, be blamed for it by people previously considered friends, colleagues and neighbours.

When, for example, a petty criminal from Tunisia drove a truck into crowds of people on the promenade in Nice on 14 July 2016, over a third of the 84 victims were Muslim. The first to die, mother of seven Fatima Charrihi, had recently completed her Ramadan fast and was, as always, wearing a hijab.

Nine months later, another Muslim woman in a headscarf was present at another vehicular terror attack, this time on Westminster Bridge in London. I don't know her name but anyone with even a passing knowledge of the social media of the time would quickly become familiar with her face. Within moments of the attack, a photograph of her looking at her phone with a clearly injured pedestrian being tended to in the background was being disseminated on Twitter and by various anti-Islamic blogs as evidence of her lack of concern for the victims.

Think, for a moment, of the fundamental presumptions and prejudices that fed the instant popularity of this profoundly false meme. First, that so many people were so keen to castigate a woman in a headscarf that they didn't even pause to wonder at the absurdity of suggesting she could be unconcerned by events that could easily have killed her. Second, the grim confidence the bloggers and tweeters had that their lies would find such a large and willing audience.

And, of course, by the time both the woman and the photographer who took the picture came forward to dismantle this vile narrative, the damage had already been done. The lie was already halfway around the world. Her words, released anonymously via the Tell Mama organisation which monitors anti-Muslim incidents, drive this point home better than I ever could.

I'm shocked and totally dismayed at how a picture of me is being circulated on social media. To those individuals who have interpreted and commented on what my thoughts were in that horrific and distressful moment, I would like to say not only have I been devastated by witnessing the aftermath of a shocking and numbing terror attack, I've also had to deal with the shock of finding my picture plastered all over social media by those who could not look beyond my attire, who draw conclusions based on hate and xenophobia.

But surely, this sort of deliberate attempt to conflate Islamist terrorists with all Muslims is something confined to crackpots in the dark corners of the internet? Unfortunately not. Just a month before the Westminster attack and following the London Bridge attack which left eight dead, the best-selling newspaper in the United Kingdom, the *Sun*, carried a comment piece under the headline 'If We Want Peace ... We Need Less Islam'*. I'm pretty sure there were people in my hometown of Kidderminster in the 1970s who would have argued that if we want peace, we need less Catholicism or, by clear implication, fewer Catholics, but thankfully I never heard them and I certainly never had to see their bigotry emblazoned across a national newspaper. Incidentally, the *Sun*'s editor at the time, Tony Gallagher, was adjudged a few months later to be the UK's sixth most prominent Catholic by the *Tablet* newspaper. We were clearly exposed to rather different interpretations of Jesus's instruction in Matthew 7:12 that we should treat others as we would like to be treated ourselves.

With vicious symmetry, that newspaper's disgraced former editor, Kelvin MacKenzie, had followed the Nice attack by questioning why a British broadcaster had allowed the story to be reported by Fatima Manji, a female Muslim newsreader who wears a headscarf. The clear implication being that a woman in a hijab, just like the first one to die beneath the wheels of the terrorist's truck, was somehow unfit to report on

---

* The *Sun*, 6/6/2017

the atrocity because of some perceived affinity with the culprit. Gallagher stood by him but MacKenzie was later dismissed as a columnist after comparing the mixed-race footballer, Ross Barkley, to a gorilla.

This context is important because it explains, and possibly partly excuses, some of the callers who have contacted me over the years apparently unaware of just how much darkness lay behind their pithily parroted assertions that 'all' Muslims are somehow responsible for acts of terror or, latterly, the despicable crimes committed by men of largely Pakistani origin in so-called grooming gangs. If these positions are being regularly expounded in the country's most popular newspapers, and reiterated in various guises on most phone-in shows and TV debates, it would be wrong to hold the consumers of such ignorant bile to a higher moral standard than those paid large sums of money to provide it.

Let's start with Richard from Marlowe, who called in January 2015 to explain why he believed all Muslims had to apologise for the attack on the offices of the French satirical magazine, *Charlie Hebdo*. Among the twelve murdered that day was Ahmed Merabet, a Muslim policeman who had raced to the scene on his bicycle before being executed in the street by one of the terrorists.

Richard is a thoughtful and clearly educated man. Listening back to this, I wonder whether I was overly aggressive, but it's important to understand that the position he expounds here was – and largely still is – going almost completely unchallenged. Indeed, the three years since the call have seen this insidious conflation move further into the mainstream and I don't understand why. Terrorists invite us to turn on each other with anger and mistrust, and this conversation demonstrates how many people in my profession and among the wider public accept that invitation with alacrity. If you were seeking to persuade an impressionable young Muslim man to become a terrorist because the 'West' really did hate him, his family and everyone like them, it's hard to think of anything more helpful to your cause than much of the media. The people who sow these bitter seeds may in part be motivated by the money on offer from the *Sun* or Fox News or other, similar outlets, but the transcript below clearly show what these seeds grow into. Richard is a poignant example. The caller immediately previous, Abbas, had rung in from Reading.

Richard: Hi James. I just want to say I agree with you up to a point, I think any reasonable person knows that most Muslims have absolutely no part in this and that it is a real and fundamental and a very, very minority group who are doing this, but I think an apology is needed. You said before that if a Geordie person had done this, should all Geordies issue an apology, and that was kind of a little bit ridiculous but ...

James: Why? Why is that any different? Why should Abbas, our last caller, apologise for what these murderers in Paris did?

Richard: Well because I think the alternative is that there is no apology.

James: Have you apologised yet?

Richard: Apologised for what?

James: The murders in France on Wednesday.

Richard: Why would I need to apologise for that?

James: Well why does Abbas? He was in Berkshire.

Richard: Well, no, because they're doing it in the name of Islam. If that was done—

James: Not his Islam. They might have been doing it in the name of Richards, wouldn't mean it was about you.

Richard: I know, but the—

James: So why haven't you apologised then? You can do it now if you want.

Richard: There has to be, there has to be some ... these people are committing acts of terror in the name of Islam.

James: Not in the name of his Islam.

Richard: I know, I do understand that.

James: So if I went and blew somebody up now, and I said I was doing this in the name of Richards everywhere, you would feel you would have to apologise? In fact, wasn't the Shoe Bomber called Richard Reid? Have you apologised for him yet?

Richard: You're making it a bit ridiculous now.

James: No, you are.

Richard: I'm really not.

James: OK, then tell me why you haven't apologised for the Shoe Bomber whose name was Richard, because Abbas has to apologise for a terrorist who said he was a Muslim? ... Take all the time you want, mate.

Richard: OK, so these guys are from the Islamic community.

James: Yes, and the Shoe Bomber was from the community of people called Richard.

Richard: We could feel some sense that some action in the Islamic community—'

James: I don't trust people called Richard anymore, so when are you going to apologise?

Richard: It is difficult to argue against you when you are being like this. I'm just trying to make a point that these people are from the Islamic community.

James: What does that even mean? What does the Islamic community even mean?

Richard: You don't understand what the Islamic community is?

James: I know that Sunni and Shia kill each other every single day in Syria on a scale that is nowhere close to what happened in France. So what do you mean by the community? You think they are on the same side, do you, those people killing each other in Syria at the moment?

Richard: No.

James: So what is the Islamic community?

Richard: The Islamic community in this country.

James: So it's just everybody who has the word 'Islam' on their religious affiliations, even if they actually hold murderous intent towards each other. Which is bringing us back to Richard, everyone who's got Richard on their passport, is part of the Richard community. You're allowed to admit you've made a mistake, my friend.

Richard: No I'm not going to admit that I've made a mistake. There needs to be a sense that we as a country—

James: I'm just going to interrupt you there Richard, which some may consider an act of mercy.

Almost three years later, in November 2017, a chap from Chester was on the line demonstrating precisely where leaving ideas like Richard's unchallenged inevitably leads. Again, I don't think Martin was a bad man and it was clear that he hated to be perceived as prejudiced or racist. By now, though, conversations around Islam had followed the path laid by Brexit and immigration and arrived at a place where having your sweeping generalisations or demonstrable wrongness about the issues pointed out would ignite a bizarre appeal to victimhood. The idea that 'freedom of speech' somehow equates with a freedom to spout undiluted, often inflammatory nonsense without being contradicted or called out is currently more popular on both sides of the Atlantic than at any other point in living memory. I believe it boils down to a simpler truth than many of us are prepared to admit to: some people are determined to believe in the fundamental badness of others. They choose to.

I seem to infuriate these people most when I insist that the crimes of a terrorist or a rapist or a paedophile are not worsened when committed by someone of a particular ethnicity or professed religion. There is a deep desire to believe that Muslims, like Jews and people of colour before them, are somehow predisposed to commit certain offences. It is a hatred as ancient as humanity itself but I never cease to be surprised by how many people don't see that they have been thoroughly caught in its clutches. As with Martin, it usually involves a swift segue from discussing people who have committed crimes to seeking to implicate people who categorically have not. I genuinely don't think they realise it's happening.

It plainly pained Martin to be perceived in this way and yet he quickly demanded the right to lump all Muslims together in precisely this fashion. And then to link them to terrorism, and then to get to determine what they all had to do to earn his approval. His position is far from exceptional.

Martin's call followed Donald Trump's decision to tweet a series of profoundly Islamophobic and/or dishonest tweets originally posted by the deputy leader of a fascist campaigning group, Britain First. The personal element of this exchange happens a lot. It can be wearing but I draw comfort from it here because it shows that he cares about my opinion. He clearly doesn't want to be considered bigoted or racist by me. Yet again, the line between what he honestly believes and where he has been unwittingly led by acres of newsprint and broadcasting is almost impossible to draw.

(You'll notice, I hope, that the three years between Richard's call and this one have taught me to be a little calmer and *slightly* less prone to interrupting!)

Martin: It sort of seems that anyone who wants to raise any concern about what's going on, you're branding them a bigot and a racist. This, that and the other.

James: Who is? Me?

Martin: That's how it comes across.

James: When I described the people responsible for recent terror attacks? I think the words I used were 'scumbags', 'disgusting' and 'beneath contempt'.

Martin: No, but anyone who wants to discuss what is going on. Let me ask you a question please.

James: Of course.

Martin: I'm half-Polish, half-Assyrian. I was born in Ghana, lived in England until I was four years old and then my father's job took us to Kuwait. I can clearly remember from that age, with no knowledge of religion or politics or anything, I did not like seeing women with their faces covered up. It scared me.

James: Same here. I don't know if it scares me but I hate it. What's the question?

Martin: The question is where are my rights? I've obeyed their rules when I lived out there, and in Saudi. Very, very, very strict Muslim countries.

James: It stinks. Medieval in the worst possible sense of the word. Now, what's the question, Martin?

Martin: Am I a bigot?

James: For what?'

Martin: I don't feel comfortable with all that.

James: Nor do I.

Martin: I would rather in this country they weren't worn.

James: I'd be uncomfortable making it a law, but I'd love for people to arrive at that conclusion independently. I just don't think laws should tell women what they can and cannot wear. But I'm closer to thinking that in this particular case a law could work than I am with any other garment. So I don't understand why you're asking whether you're a bigot for agreeing with me on all of these issues.

Martin: I'm concerned, as I say. Shall we say we have had a lot more terrorism going on in the last few years and it has all come from a particular group?

James: Not compared to the seventies or the eighties.

(He sighs heavily here and blows what sounds like a small raspberry.)

James: That's just called counting, mate. So again, what's the question? You've asked 'Am I a bigot?' and I don't understand what you think you've said that might leave you open to an accusation of bigotry.

Martin: I want to discuss the fact that, having lived out in Saudi and the Middle East, my personal view is that there is an overriding thing that they do want to take over. It was openly said that 'We want the whole world to be Muslim.'

James: OK. And the fact that we arm this particular regime and make excuses for them in Parliament and beyond is a source of immense national shame, but I still don't understand what it is you think you're not allowed to say without being labelled. The Saudi royal family would arguably have been toast years ago if it wasn't for the support of the British government. But you did use me as an example. You seem to think that I am going to call you a bigot for saying things I've said a million times myself.

Martin: Well it does seem as if anyone who wants to talk about—

James: You can't keep saying that, Martin, when everything you've said so far I've agreed with. The face veil is, to my mind, appallingly oppressive and wrong. The notion of Saudi supremacy in the Middle East seems to me be the source of an awful lot of what's going wrong in the world. So go on, mate. What do you think you're not allowed to say?

Martin: My standpoint is that I am concerned about the Muslim population in this country. That there are actually more, shall we say, supporting things than there would be at face value. And you actually had a guy on yesterday which I think really highlighted it. He was asked why he wouldn't assimilate into life in the UK and his whole attitude was 'Why should I assimilate?'

James: I don't know what you're talking about now, Martin.

Martin: It wasn't your programme.

Martin: Right. So you heard a bloke on a phone-in show, who to my mind sounds like a bit of a berk, and that makes you think we should all be more terrorised by Muslims who probably support terrorists but don't publicly declare it?

Martin: That's the basic thing.

James: OK. Well, you've said that now.

Martin: But presenters like yourself try to put it that the problem is very, very, very small.

James: No. Presenters like myself are trying to explain that the scale of a problem is determined and defined by things that have happened.

Martin: No, your rhetoric basically says that the problem is very small.

James: Martin, it really doesn't. How can anyone be in denial about a terror attack? What you're claiming is that we should be more terrorised by people who haven't done anything wrong yet because there's a strong likelihood that they might.

Martin: I think we should be more *concerned* than we are.

James: But how can we be more concerned? It's by far the biggest issue of national security facing the security services at the moment.

Martin: Well, this is how it comes across on your programme.

James: So what you've rung in to say is that you heard some bloke on somebody else's programme on this radio station yesterday and that proves something about me that you want to believe.

Martin: No. What I'm trying to say, if you could just listen and stop trying to be clever about everything—

James: Mate, I'm already two and a half minutes late for the news. I can hardly give you more freedom of speech.

Martin: You always feel you have to be right and have the last word.

James: I've agreed with you, though. I've agreed with every word you've said. Apart from the bit about being frightened of people who haven't actually done anything wrong. I don't agree with that because, well, that way leads to thought police, doesn't it?

Martin: Well, that's what we have actually got, the thought police. People are too afraid to speak out.

James: OK. And you want more of that, do you? You want more policing of what you think people think rather than what they've actually done or said?

Martin: What I would like to see is more people in that group weeding out their own bad apples. That's what we don't see and I think that's what upsets a lot of people.

James: But what if they don't think they're in the same group. Any more than I bear responsibility for the actions of the IRA or you are somehow responsible for the crimes of white paedophiles. Would you say that you were in the same group as them?

Martin: It would be nice to see more members of the Muslim community doing more to weed out their bad apples. We don't see that and that's where the concern lies.

James: OK. And you still think that by saying that out loud you somehow become a bigot in the eyes of people like me?

Martin: That's how I feel.

James: OK. Well I cannot help how you feel. You know how this programme works. We deal in facts and evidence. And all of the facts, all of the evidence today suggest that what you've just said does not leave you exposed to an accusation of bigotry. Your examples about Saudi Arabia, your examples about face veils, I would agree with. I would describe them [face veils] as medievalist, backwards and wrong. But you're determined to be more terrorised, Martin. That seems to be what you want. You want us to be more terrorised. And the best way to do that is to take loads and loads of completely innocent Muslims and tell them that they're somehow responsible for terrorists, for atrocities and carnage. They're no more responsible for that than you are but you're not comfortable with this argument because you want people to be more terrorised. And so do the terrorists, mate. So, in terms of that simple question: do you want people to be more or less terrorised, your answer is ...'

Martin: Less terrorised.

James: OK. Well, that's your choice. You can choose right now to be less terrorised and the best way to start would be to stop claiming that all Muslims are somehow complicit in acts of terror. And then, immediately, you'd be confining your anger and your fear to people who commit acts of terror and not the people who sell you milk in the morning, do your accounts or drive you home at night after a skinful. Because they're all Muslims and they've got no more to do with terrorism than you have. So you're on the same side as them. Do you see?

Martin: It's a very difficult subject.

James: It really isn't. You're making it difficult and people like Donald Trump and the Islamic State love the difficulty that you're having because it feeds the hatred they're seeking to spread. You choose whether or not you're going to be a tool of that hatred.

I wonder now whether that's really true. If Martin, like many others, has fallen down a largely internet-based rabbit hole of race hate and Islamophobia, can he really choose to be unaffected by it? The reason why conversations like this are simultaneously so frustrating and revealing is that people like him have lost the desire to question what they are being told. Their bespoke, unchallenged diet of 'news', augmented we now know by Facebook algorithms and deliberately fake stories, is so unvaried that the possibility that it might be largely bogus is never entertained. It's also worth pointing out here how easy it is to confine criticism of face veils to the garment rather than the human being wearing one. When the former Foreign Secretary, Boris Johnson, elected to compare these human beings to 'bank robbers' and 'letterboxes' in August 2018*, he was feeding the anger and confusion of people like Martin. It's hard to imagine what good he thought might come of it.

One of the most memorable calls I have ever taken came during the brief heyday of the so-called English Defence League. This ragtag bunch of football hooligans realised quicker than most that with newspapers in decline and trust in traditional media vulnerable to attack from all sides, some people would enjoy being told, repeatedly and furiously, about the enemy within; the fifth column who could not be easily identified. They

---

* *Daily Telegraph*, 6/8/2018

demanded that anyone who *might* be an Islamist terrorist – i.e. pretty much everyone who's Muslim or even brown – should be treated with suspicion and contempt.

Ray was, I guess, in his early sixties and a little nervous at the outset. The conversation that morning had been about people who actively choose to be frightened and angry and spend hours searching for more nourishment online every day. It was prompted by one of my oldest friends who had started watching videos online and reading the EDL website and ended up quite convinced that Muslims were his enemy, despite not actually knowing any. He showed me 'summaries' of Koranic texts posted as proof that any Muslim who claimed not to want to see all infidels driven into the sea was somehow not a 'proper' Muslim. This rhetoric is deftly designed to feed the suspicions that people like Martin have of all Muslims.

Ray: I was just listening to what you said about the internet melting our brains and I wanted to tell you what happened to me.

James: Go on.

Ray: I don't really know any Muslims, but I started reading stuff online a few months ago, the EDL and that, and the more I read the angrier I got.

James: Angry about what?

Ray: Angry about these people poncing off us while plotting to kill us.

James: Wow.

Ray: I know, but they'd back it up by quoting from the Koran or the Hadiths and kind of prove all their points about Muslims without ever actually talking to any.

James: So what happened?

Ray: My wife told me to stop.

James: What do you mean?

Ray: I was getting angry with her, with the family, with everyone really. I'd start trying to convince everyone that we were under siege and they just couldn't see it. The wife said I was making myself ill and making her unhappy and she told me to leave the laptop under the sofa for a month.

James: What happened?

Ray: I was sorted in less than a week. Never look at that stuff anymore. Couldn't be happier.

I love calls like this because they reinforce my increasingly desperate hope that things are a lot easier than they sometimes appear. If people like Ray, or my old mate, can be encouraged to lift their heads out of their laptops and ask themselves whether they can actually see any cause for concern in their real lives, they will be a lot better off for it. As would, of course, the entirely innocent people they have been encouraged to be suspicious of.

There are Islamist extremists, of course there are. There are also men of largely Pakistani origin who can be fairly described as Muslim and who have been responsible for the gang-rape and abuse of hundreds of young women in towns like Telford and Rotherham on an epidemic scale. But neither of these grim constituencies represent anyone but themselves. The leaching into the mainstream news that they somehow provide proof that Muslims are fundamentally different from the rest of us – or that they remain committed to the destruction of a society their forebears crossed the world to join – is as daft as it is dangerous. But the problem is a lot bigger now than it was when I started reporting it. Only when you consider that a website like Breitbart, which exists pretty much exclusively to foment precisely the fear and anger detailed here, was run by the man who became Donald Trump's campaign manager do you appreciate how far into the public discourse this poison has travelled.

So who benefits? Well, white supremacist rhetoric is clearly resurgent and some people really do seem to believe in its ideology. Invariably, they personally represent the worst imaginable arguments in favour of any notion of a 'master race', but then Hitler was hardly the embodiment of his own Aryan dream. Hand on heart, I don't know whether some of the more prominent educated, middle-class names in the hate dissemination industry, the Milos and the Hopkinses, really believe in what they are selling but they certainly believe in the fame and, to a lesser extent, the fortune that their preaching can bring. I don't know what's worse, doing it for money while not believing in it or doing it because you really do believe that ethnicity and geography deliver some sort of innate value to a human being.

But be in no doubt about where it all leads. It leads to Frank, from Birkenhead, who I would once have written off as an extremist loon but who now represents a real and growing group of people who don't have a wife like Ray's, or any desire to seek the sort of harmony and fellowship that, before doing this job, I used to think we almost all yearned for. Frank's arguments, incidentally, were almost identical to the ones that my EDL-loving friend would employ whenever I attempted to challenge the pictures being painted for him in internet chatrooms.

Frank: We need to close the mosques and we need to ban the Koran and we need to recognise that Islam is a takeover movement.

James: But these people will still be here if we close all the mosques, Frank. We're burning books now, I guess, and closing places of worship but all these people will still be here. What are we going to do with them?

Frank: James, I'd rather burn books than see people burned to death by bombs and guns.

James: What are we going to do with all these people?

Frank: Well, let's do what you want to do. Let all the Muslims take over.

James: I'm asking what you want to do. Stop talking about me all the time!

Frank: OK. We stop them coming in.

James: But what do we do with the ones that are here, Frank?

Frank: We ask them this question: 'Do you believe in jihad? Do you believe in killing for Allah?'

I cannot stress enough how prevalent this is, or how much effort has been put into making people like Frank believe that a 'proper' Muslim is somehow committed to killing or converting him. It's like a parallel universe where every Facebook post, every 'freedom of speech' march, every Fox News contributor complaining that terrorism isn't terrorising enough people is dedicated to making people like Frank feel under existential threat. Muslim listeners generally respond to calls like this by pointing out that they're too busy doing the school run to be waging war against the *kuffir*. Or that they were going to do a bit of jihad, but something good dropped on Netflix. It is, for my money, the British way to respond to such misguided fury – with disarming humour, but Donald Trump and Steve Bannon have shown what a powerful political force that misguided fury can be when properly harnessed.

James: And you think they'll say yes.

Frank: No.

James: So what do we do with all the ones who say no? The ones who don't cough immediately to being secret jihadists, hellbent upon destroying Western civilisation.

Frank: What we have to do, James, is very easy. We have to say to them: if you want to be part of this society, you must reject jihad.

James: But what if they just lie? How can you trust them?

(This, of course, was also a fatal flaw in Trump's stated plan to somehow prevent Muslims from entering the United States. For reasons I still struggle to understand, its patent impossibility rarely dilutes the enthusiasm of its supporters.)

Frank: You have to fit in with Christianity. No one kills for Jesus. With Buddhism, no one kills for Buddha. With Chinese faith, no one kills for Confucius.

James: There are atrocities being undertaken in the name of Buddha in Burma as we speak, Frank, and you'd struggle to argue that a belief in Jesus has never contributed to any wars or terrorism. Even the Irish Troubles are ostensibly about two different flavours of the same Christianity. But what are we going to do with them, because I think they'll all lie, won't they? They'll all say they reject jihad, so what do we do next?

Frank: Well, we have to put them to the test, don't we?

James: How do we do that? How do we put them to the test?

Frank: We ask them, are you going to reject this faith?

James: But they'll probably lie, Frank. What do we do next after they've lied?

Frank: What we do next, is we take the Koran off them and we burn the Koran because that is what teaches them to mass murder.

James: OK. But what do we do with the people after we've burned all the books?

Frank: Well, ultimately, there's an Islamic world. If they want to practise their Islamic faith, let them go back to their Islamic countries and stop killing us.

Frank gets quite angry now. It's par for the course. He's not, however, angry because he is being prevented from speaking his mind, which is the usual dishonest complaint. He's angry because he has spoken his mind but has now been asked to explain himself; he is being asked to think. The conflation of 'freedom of speech' with 'freedom to say silly things without being challenged' and, more, 'freedom to insist that people have to listen to me even if they think I'm ridiculous and/or dangerous' is rarely quite as glaring as in this case.

James: Frank, it's not my fault this isn't going well for you. Just shouting at me isn't going to improve things.

Frank: You just mock, James. You're a liar.

James: So. To recap. You ask these people to condemn jihad. They say that they do but we don't believe them, so we somehow deport them to countries they've never been to? Is that the plan?

Frank: If they say they condemn jihad they cease to be Muslims so they don't need a mosque and they don't need a Koran. If they want to be Muslims let them go back to the Islamic world. Let them kill each other as long as they stop killing us.

James: Well we got there in the end, Frank. You don't think we can live together in peace. Neither does Isis. You are doing the work of the terrorists and I guess, in a way, it's helpful to hear it so bold and so cold. In answer to my question of what you want to do with these people, you have absolutely nothing. But you don't really care, Frank, as long as you can keep the hatred alive.

See what I mean? For Frank, and I suspect for millions like him, there is no distinction any more between someone simply practising their faith and a killer-in-waiting. If you are a Muslim you want to kill people like him, whether you realise it or not. It sounds a little extreme but if there is a better explanation for his fearful fury then I am yet to unearth it.

I may have not *completely* won Frank over during our conversation, but it really was helpful to see his thinking laid out so clearly. He holds precisely the same position as all the prominent people on Infowars and Breitbart or those peddling their home-made videos online who routinely claim that their freedom to say such things is being compromised – usually while inviting financial contributions from their deluded flocks. Their problem is not that they are in any way prevented from preaching the sort of ignorant hatred Frank espoused, their problem is with people like me – and hopefully you – remaining free to describe it as ignorant hatred and, even more infuriatingly, being capable of proving it.

Chapter 2
BREXIT

I STILL DON'T KNOW what they think they won. This is an odd, perhaps even embarrassing, admission because I've been asking 'Leavers' what change they most desired to see in their lives or country for years. Long before David Cameron's towering hubris saw the referendum on EU membership become a reality in 2016, I was frequently baffled by people convinced that they were subject to a whole raft of oppressive and restrictive laws inflicted upon them by 'unelected bureaucrats in Brussels' but who were at the same time uniformly unable to name a single one that they were looking forward to losing.

Although, that may not be entirely fair. I remember in about 2010, long before the age of viral clips and online 'dismantlings' saw such exchanges reach far beyond the radio, a Ukip MEP rang in to put me straight where callers were once again struggling. There were, he insisted, 'loads' of laws that left us unjustifiably enslaved to the EU. Indeed, there were 'too many to list'. Pushed to name just one, specifically and repeatedly, he left the field after spluttering, prevaricating, patronising and, finally, explaining that EU food refrigeration regulations could compromise the freedom of the Women's Institute to hold cake sales.

It's possible, I suppose, that this is both true and sufficient grounds for leaving the largest free market the world has ever seen, but it seems unlikely, to say the least. More plausible, unfortunately, is the idea that the whole debate never received deep scrutiny because many people who would later be derided as 'experts' couldn't quite believe that they needed to publicly win arguments with such numbskulls, and by the time they realised that nonsensical notions really did need to be debated seriously, it was too late.

Fast forward seven years, and the achingly narrow victory for Leave was transmogrifying into an amorphous 'will of the people'. This 'will', apparently, meant that 17.4 million disparate and diverse people had all voted for exactly the same thing without realising it: namely, a Brexit which would mean whatever Paul Dacre, the billionaire owners of the *Daily Telegraph* and Jacob Rees-Mogg wanted it to. It's hard to know which hypocrisy highlights this best, but I was particularly struck by the speed with which people who had insisted, quite deceitfully, that 'we' had only voted to join a trading bloc in 1975, then started insisting furiously that we had knowingly and deliberately voted to leave that trading bloc, the customs union and the single market in 2016.

Dacre's *Daily Mail* led the unprecedented onslaught of vitriol directed at anyone who dared to question the direction of travel or demanded to know more about the eventual destination. For a self-styled defender of 'British values' it was remarkable to observe how quickly his incoherent rage was directed at venerable and deeply valuable British institutions. Three front-page headlines in the aftermath of the result attacked, respectively, the independence of the judiciary ('Enemies of the People'), the ability of elected MPs to do their democratic duty ('Crush the Saboteurs'), and even academic freedom ('Our Remainer Universities'). He is, thankfully, no longer in the editor's chair but his nation-damaging legacy will continue to pollute public discourse for at least a generation.

Consider also the shameful redrawing of positions that was undertaken by prominent Brexiters as reality began to bite. They went, in the space of just two years, from arguing that 'the EU needs us more than we need them' to 'it should be the easiest deal in human history'. Next, as negotiations proved impervious to blind optimism they segued from 'no deal is better than a bad deal' to 'the EU must believe that we're prepared to walk away without any deal so that we can get a good deal'. It all culminated, inevitably, in an attempt to somehow frame the EU's preparation for the no-deal scenario 'we' had threatened them with as evidence of their intransigence and ill will. And if we thought their ignorance of the single market and customs union was spectacular – the Conservative MP Nadine Dorries famously sought advice from colleagues on what the former actually was because she was struggling to win an argument about why it was so important to leave it[*] – it began to look positively encyclopaedic when they moved on to 'explaining' how the World Trade Organisation functions.

And all because of those pesky EU laws. Just like the Ukip MEP's doughty defence of theoretical cakes, people have been telling me for years that the EU restricted their freedoms and imposed undesirable laws. And, for years, they have proved to be uniformly incapable of naming one. I must have asked dozens of times and faced the same cod answers: the conflation of the European Court of Human Rights with the European Parliament; the lazy and erroneous depiction of the EU Commission's structure as being somehow less 'democratic' than our relationship with our own Parliament, civil service and Cabinet, and the final, desperate appeals to 'blue passports' and 'fish!'

Andy from Nottingham was a particularly painful example. By October 2016 I was quietly despairing that the gaping holes in Brexiters' accounts of what was going to happen next were never going to be filled. It was becoming almost surreal to see people like Nigel Farage retreat from previously stated positions and claim that the mandate achieved after suggesting that we could be like Norway or Switzerland would somehow still apply when the Prime Minister insisted that the 'will of the people' had determined we could be nothing like Norway or Switzerland.

After the referendum, it had at first been funny, albeit perhaps a little cruel, to lead people gently to the realisation that they had

[*] Buzzfeed, 27/1/2018

been spectacularly silly, but by now it was downright depressing and not a little horrifying. By this point, many of us could see that anger was best reserved for the people who were still selling the snake oil, as opposed to the punters who had guzzled it.

Andy, a plumber, began by explaining that he had cast his vote knowing that there would be a 'short-term, personal financial loss'.

> **Andy:** I recently went self-employed a couple of years ago so it was a big thing voting Brexit because I was building my business, but I think it's all going to be short-term.
>
> **James:** What is?
>
> **Andy:** The personal financial loss.

At this point, it's worth remembering that the vast majority of prominent Brexiters dismissed warnings of any economic harm from Brexit as Project Fear, and in many cases insisted that there wouldn't be any. My personal favourite, for want of a better word, is Andrea Leadsom, who revealed a week before the vote that: 'My best expectation, with my 30 years of financial experience, is that there will not be an economic impact.'

A week after the vote she was mounting a credible campaign to replace David Cameron as Conservative leader and prime minister. Four months after that, in the very month that Andy called me, she had been installed as Environment Secretary and was explaining to a trade fair in Paris that 'British jam, tea and biscuits' would be at the heart of Britain's Brexit trade negotiations.

So back to Andy:

James: To be fair, they did tell you before the vote that there wouldn't be any [personal financial loss].

Andy: Well, I believed there would be and I was willing to take that sacrifice just for the independence and so that we would control our own laws.

James: You know what I do now, don't you?

Andy: What's that?

James: I ask you which law it is you're really looking forward to not having to obey any more.

Andy: Well, any ...?

James: That's right, any. So give me one.

Andy: Errrrrm ... the shape of your bananas?

He laughs nervously; I can't. It's not always easy to remember that anger should be directed at the dupers as opposed to the duped, but on this occasion it was simple enough.

James: It's not funny is it? The pound's the lowest it's been since 1985 and I just asked you to name any law, just one, and you say bananas. We both know that the bananas line was a lie made up by Boris Johnson. Remind me which side he was on?'

Andy: Well, he was out for himself.

See? Andy is not stupid. He's a bright, entrepreneurial professional with his own young company and an eye on the future. He hasn't mentioned immigration (yet) and doesn't subscribe to some bogus nineteenth-century notion of English exceptionalism. He has – and this is crucial to understand – simply existed for years in a media-defined environment where the depiction of the overarching and negative influence of 'EU laws' went so unchallenged it became, for him and millions like him, a simple truth. Citing bendy bananas didn't prove a lack of substantive evidence for his position, rather it proved how deeply ingrained it had become in much of the national psyche that bananas were somehow the tip of some malevolent iceberg. If what followed seems unkind or even condescending (I don't think it does but it's a common criticism), please try to distinguish between the people who led him into this mess and the person now trying to lead him out of it.

James: So what is the law, Andy? Because you knew you were going to suffer short-term damage, you knew that all your customers were going to ... So I'm just wondering what the laws were, that you won't have to obey any more, that made you vote for this short-term economic hit?

Andy: Well, it wasn't the laws which was the main reason ...

James: It was the main reason you gave me, wasn't it, just a minute ago?

Andy: Yeah ...

James: Can you name one yet?

Andy: I wouldn't be able to. No.

James: So you voted so that you wouldn't have to obey these EU laws that you can't name?

Andy: No, no. It's more than that.

James: Well, go on ...

Andy: You go to Brussels, you watch the guys talking. It's all very ... it's very political. They're throwing their toys out of the pram because, you know, the British people chose to leave. It's like baking a cake and taking into work and someone says they don't want a slice and they get all uppity about it ...

James: We're trying to work out why you voted the way you voted. Because you now accept it's going to cost you money, you *hope* in the short term. I hate to break it to you, but we're not even going to be close to signing new trade deals for years so that uncertainty that's affecting your order book is going to continue indefinitely. And I asked you why you did it, why you accepted that hit to your own pocket, and you say because of all those laws that you can't name, and when I ask you what the real reason is you say because the EU is really political. At what point, as I hold this mirror up – are you going to recognise what you're seeing? You're seeing a man who hasn't got an argument.

And then, as it almost always does ...

Andy: There are multiple arguments. There's immigration ... I'm not, you know, I'm not xenophobic. I'm totally multicultural. I've got family in America, in Bermuda, in Spain. Immigrants are fine. They're the same as me and you, trying to do their best for their family, but it's not about that – it's about the control. It's about our Prime Minister having to succumb to the EU saying that he can't or she can't do anything.

James: That's fine. I've got no beef with you. If immigration's all you've got, you're the cliché. You're the walking cliché. What's interesting, Andy, and I hope you won't take this the wrong way, is that you spend five minutes pretending that you've got political or economic arguments and as all of those fall away you're just left with foreigners.

Andy: No. No. Definitely not.

James: How has immigration damaged your life would you say?

Andy: Well, obviously, being in a trade, immigration has pulled prices down

James: No, not as a qualified plumber. There's scant evidence [from the Bank of England in 2015] that immigration effected some wage compression in the completely unskilled labour market but there's actually a shortage of qualified plumbers in this country, which is probably why you've gone self-employed. So it's not that, is it? So, just in terms of Andy in Nottingham and the damage that uncontrolled mass immigration has done to your life, just give me the headline.

Andy: Um. Walking through the city centre and seeing mobs of, um, of immigrants not willing to integrate.

James: And how do you think leaving the European Union is going to disperse those mobs, Andy?

Andy: I think we'll have more control—

James: They're already here, mate.

Andy: Yeah, but we'll have more control—

James: But they're here. Those mobs that upset you so much as you wander through town and see those mobs of immigrants refusing to integrate, now that we're going to leave the European Union, what's going to happen to the mobs?

[Pause]

Andy: Um. I believe that we can, we can, we can integrate them because I believe that, you know, we have the choice and we have the, um, we have the authority to do what we like without, you know, without human rights being involved …

James: So you've cast your vote because you think there are too many of these people here and you think that by doing that you're going to make them more amenable to integration and friendliness. So you deliver a message to someone saying we don't like you and you think that makes them more likely to be your friend?

Andy: It's not about liking anyone.

> **James:** Well, you don't like the mobs in the middle of town, do you?
>
> **Andy:** No. No, and that goes with mobs of Englishmen as well. It's not a matter of race.
>
> **James:** So it's got nothing to do with immigration, then? It's just mobs you don't like.

He laughs again here. I like Andy. I still don't think he's racist. I feel a bit bad at feeding him so much rope. He's been hearing the views he's espousing here for years without ever having heard them challenged before. It's not a popular view – and this may actually *be* patronising – but I honestly don't think any of this is his fault.

> **Andy:** Yeah, I just don't like mobs!
>
> **James:** And bananas. And all those laws that you can't name.

We part, chuckling, with his view that the economic harm he's already suffering will last fewer than five years and that, even if all of his potential customers are similarly affected, it would still, somehow, be 'worth it'. I sincerely hope his business is booming.

It is impossible to stop people claiming that Andy was sneered at here, or condescended to, or that his final, desperate reaching for immigrant mobs blighting Nottingham city centre is somehow evidence that all 'Remainers' think all 'Leavers' are racist or stupid. It would be nonsense on stilts, of course, but that doesn't stop it being a highly effective way of shutting down criticism. I have, on more than occasion, completed a brief explanation of how many Leave voters I know personally – friends, family, colleagues – only to be told by the very next caller that I believe all Leave voters to be racist or stupid, or both.

Ultimately, it discourages thinking. Instead, we are encouraged to pick our side based on either decades of deliberately deceitful depictions of the EU as a meddlesome Fourth Reich or on carefully cultivated fears of the country being overrun by foreigners. We then stick to it regardless. Phrases like 'Take Back Control' and words like 'sovereignty', or even 'anglo-sphere', sound meaningful and can be wheeled out in debate and conversation as some sort of glittering prizes. But they are, it has become clear, entirely hollow. If you don't think about things you will never understand them, but with a couple of clever-sounding soundbites you might kid yourself – and others – that you do. This criticism is not confined to callers like Andy. It goes to the very top of the Brexit machine.

At the same time, if you can somehow portray anyone asking a person to account for their opinions, to explain their beliefs, as some sort of 'out-of-touch elite' who secretly thinks they're addressing a stupid racist, then you invalidate their questions and excuse people from trying to answer them. I realise now that the biggest threat to Brexit is asking people to describe the thought processes that led them to their voting preference. It's a shame hardly anybody was doing it before the referendum.

Theresa May took this aversion to thinking to its apotheosis when she declared that 'Brexit means Brexit' shortly after becoming prime minister in July 2016. Even by the standards of modern British politics, this is a slogan of such sweeping vacuity that it beggars belief that she could utter the words with a straight face. Ask yourself now what it actually means. Consider the events of the following months and years and ask yourself whether she could have been doing anything other than using it to discourage thinking, to avoid facts and to postpone reality. You don't need to be William of Ockham to conclude that this is the *only* – never mind the simplest – explanation for her choice of words.

The truly nasty element of the whole enterprise is the way it treats the Brexit-supporting British public as idiots. Throw them a fatuous soundbite, the thinking goes, and they'll be so busy chomping away on it that they won't notice we haven't got the first idea what Brexit is going to mean. So go ahead and malign dissenters as sneering elites; typify criticism as an accusation of racism and castigate questions as unpatriotic. It worked for a while, but by December 2017, the mask was slipping and callers like Sean in Uxbridge revealed what often happened when Leave voters were robustly encouraged to explain the thinking behind their vote. Think of Sean as a poster boy for people who talk about 'legitimate concerns' surrounding immigration and dismiss the notion that this is often just camouflage for some pretty base views.

Sean: I've been here for 30 years and when I walk into Uxbridge I swear to God I don't know where I am. I've got Polish, Romanians, Bulgarians sitting outside coffee houses doing sod all, all day. When I go into hospital, I walk into A&E and out of 120 people I'm lucky if I see three or four white faces.

James: Now, that is racist.

Sean: No it isn't. It's realistic.

James: It really is. That last bit is because you're forming an opinion of people, of their value, based on their colour. There are people who don't have white faces who are just as British as you and me, Sean.

Sean: Perhaps they are, James, but—

James: No. They really are, Sean. Let's not do this. Let's do it nicely. Just tell me the European Union country that is populated by mostly non-white people.

[Pause]

Sean: Couldn't tell you.

James: Well, have a go. Have a little think.

Sean: Say the question again.

James: The European Union member that has a mostly non-white population. Because we're talking about your reasons for wanting to leave the European Union and you mentioned the number of non-white people at your local hospital, so which European Union countries are essentially non-white?

[Pause]

Sean: Probably none.

James: So why are you talking about those people then?

Sean: Alright. Alright. Let's backtrack.

James: Let's do that, mate. I'm happy to let you do that.

Sean: It is still a valid point, James.

James: Not in the context of a conversation about the EU it's not, and I say this with love and reluctance, Sean, but if you are judging people according to the colour of their skin then you are indulging in racial prejudice. You see, I don't care what colour *you* are, I'm never going to say to the producer at the end of the programme that we had too many black people on today or too many white people.

Sean: It's not all about ... it's not all about white people. Look, we're going off on a tangent here.

James: No, you did mate. I'm just reining you back in again.

Sean: It's not all about the racist issue. It's just that the country has lost its identity.

James: What does that mean?

Sean: Well, what does it mean? It means what I've just said.

James: You've just said that you don't like seeing brown faces at the hospital.

Sean: Alright then, I'll give you another example. I might be digging myself a big hole here ...

James: I'll pull you out, mate, I promise.

Sean: Alright. I'll give you an absolute point here. If you went down to my local supermarket where my two sons tried to get jobs in between college and university ... at one point, James, out of 23 tills, Indian or Pakistani people were behind 22 of them.

James: We're talking about the European Union, Sean.

Sean: But what I'm trying to say, James, is that this is where it's all coming from. Because when I mentioned this to the manager he said they had to reflect the whole community. Now is that right, James? That is why people have voted out of Europe.

James: Because we've got too many brown people on the tills in Uxbridge?

Sean: No, it's not about too many brown people.

James: Sean, if it's not about that, why do you keep talking about how many brown people there are in the hospital and the supermarket?

Sean: Because that is why people voted to leave Europe.

James: I completely agree with you. A lot of people voted that way because they're frightened of brown people.

Sean: No, it's not about that James.

James: Help me out here, because I can kind of get my head around some of it. I work on the phones every day. I generally have no idea what colour anybody is. Why does it matter to you what colour the person that you buy your milk off is?

Sean: It doesn't matter what colour they are. The point I'm trying to make is why people voted out of Europe.

James: I completely agree with you. They voted out because they think there are too many brown people in some towns.

For all the subsequent hand-wringing and revisionism, every single person who campaigned to leave the EU knew full well that they were feeding prejudices like Sean's. They can claim to abhor Nigel Farage's despicable 'Breaking Point' poster until they're blue in the face, but history will record how happy they were to harvest any votes it secured. It will take ages for this particular genie to be put back in the bottle and, whatever transpires with regard to Brexit, the revivification of racist abuse and discrimination will be with us for years to come. I can't tell you whether that will make Sean's world a happier one or whether his sense of 'identity' will be in any way enhanced, but I can tell you that the way to address his 'legitimate concerns' is not to quietly nod and express sympathetic understanding. It is to treat him like an intelligent, thoughtful human being and so encourage him to understand the origins and implications of the views he holds. My job is to hold up a mirror while he's doing it.

Just over a year after the referendum, Dean in Epping Forest provided further evidence of just how effectively people had been groomed to see a vote to leave as a vote to somehow reduce the number of foreigners in their midst. The Liberal

Democrat leader, Vince Cable, had opined that morning that Leave voters would start to regret their decision as they saw increasing evidence of how they had been misled. I sadly disagreed, and Dean helped me show why.

Dean: I don't believe it was about economics. I believe it was solely about immigration. And if there is a slight downturn, then I believe that's a small price to pay for controlling your own borders and making your own laws.

James: And when you have it explained to you that, under current European Union law, it's perfectly possible for member states to deport citizens of other member countries if they haven't found work after three months or if they cannot demonstrate that they have sufficient capital to sustain their lives here; when it's explained to you factually that the whole 'controlling our borders' argument was utterly bogus – just go to Belgium and try to set yourself up over there as a Brit – then what happens?

This refers to Article 7 of the EU Citizens' Rights Directive. You may wonder why you weren't previously aware of it or, if you were, why it hasn't featured more prominently in the debate. I was ignorant of it. It's no excuse but it's an explanation that I suspect applies to almost everyone in my profession who sought to be either impartial or to encourage a Remain vote. It genuinely never occurred to us that the most central platform of Brexit rhetoric – that freedom of movement was utterly untrammelled and uncontrollable – was demonstrably untrue. It's important to remember that David Cameron and his Home Secretary Theresa May had weaponised immigration electorally with such success that, by the time of the 2015 election, the Labour Party had aped some of their rhetoric. Neither party was minded to explain that enacting Article 7 would be uneconomical and largely pointless because the 'sponging EU migrant' was largely mythical. There aren't any votes in tackling tabloid tropes about non-existent or grossly exaggerated problems. I mention this because, while he may not be as immediately deserving of sympathy as Andy or even Sean, Dean can't be blamed for not knowing this. What upsets me most about Dean's call, and hundreds like it, is that he's been led by the nose into a position of dangerous ignorance, but he will end up crosser with the people who point it out to him than he will ever be with the people who did the leading.

> **Dean:** Well, the way I look at it is that, I lived in Australia for a few years and if I wanted to go back to Australia I would have to prove I could speak English, I'd have to have a certain amount in the bank, I'd have to have medical tests. I'd have to have a skill that is on a list of what they need. And why can't we apply those things here?

This, of course, is the 'Australian Points System' that politicians and pundits had been allowed to cite for years without proper challenge or reference to the aforementioned Article 7. It applies to a very different set of demographic and economic circumstances than we have in the UK but is perceived as very stringent and so supported by many people like Dean. It has not, of course, effected any decrease in the number of Australian Deans who still opine that their country has a massive problem with incomers. Politically, it allows governments to demonstrate how harshly they are treating potential immigrants but it demonstrably does not dilute anti-immigrant feeling. A giant red herring, in other words.

James: But I've just told you that we can be a lot more robust. Like they do in Belgium. Like they do in Germany. So when it's been explained to you that it was successive British governments who failed or elected not to enact laws, so the whole 'control our borders' argument falls to pieces, at that point Vince Cable thinks people will realise they were wrong. What is Vince Cable missing? Why aren't people bright enough to realise they were wrong when they're presented with incontrovertible evidence that the borders argument was bogus, Dean? Obviously, the main reason why British governments haven't done more to control the movement of labour is because it would cost more than it could ever hope to save, what with EU migrants being net contributors to the economy.

Dean: You might well be right.

James: I am right. So why do people like you still insist that the vote was about the absence of immigration controls?

Dean: Three months is too long.

James: So how are we going to cope with holidays?

Dean: You need a holiday visa to go to Australia.

James: So what are we going to need to go to France?

Dean: I don't know. I don't really want to go to France.

James: Or Germany or Spain or Italy or Greece?

Dean: No.

James: Well, that's the point isn't it? When I ask what Vince Cable's missing, he's missing the existence of people like you who don't want to go to France and think that that's a political position.

[Pause]

Dean: Yeah. Maybe.

James: And in terms of being demonstrably poorer, that's good thing because …?

Dean: Well, I don't believe that will happen. We possibly may have a dip for a few years but I think in the long run we'll be fine.

It still amazes me that only a year after the vote, people who were still happy that Britain is leaving the EU had already been reduced to presenting 'in the long run, I think we'll be fine' as some sort of victory. And again, while it's easy to mock Dean, his position is no different to that of prominent politicians who would, if they were ever properly pressed on the issue, have little option but to offer Dean's answer to my next question.

James: What do you base that on?

Dean: That's just my belief.

James: But what do you base it on?

Dean: Well, I haven't got any hard, scientific facts in front of me.

James: Just give me some soft, unscientific facts then.

Dean: Well, we used to own three thirds of the world.

James: Three thirds?

Dean: Sorry, two thirds of the world and we are, you know, a massive trading country.

I still don't know what they think they won. And, despite being adamant that day that the existence of people like Dean would give the lie to Vince Cable's optimism, I still don't know why buyer's remorse didn't set in harder and faster. The best available explanation is that European Union debates in the UK have for decades been more psychological than political. My attempts to shine a light into the dark corners of minds like Dean's were mostly doomed because he, and many others, remain psychologically incapable of entertaining the possibility that the EU might not be malevolent.

If someone tells you, apparently in good faith, that an organisation or individual is dedicated to damaging your existence, in the very first instance there are only three possible responses: you ignore or dismiss the claim completely; you believe it immediately and come out swinging, or you examine the evidence and respond accordingly.

I think most people in the United Kingdom spent years subscribing almost exclusively to the first and second options and this, more than anything else, explains how we ended up where we ended up. Our reactions have been intuitive and emotional as opposed to evidential and intellectual. Crucially, and contrary to most analysis, under this reading both sides are guilty of the same offence: picking a position and sticking to it without doing the heavy lifting needed to make it truly secure. On the one side, the very thought of membership prompted impassioned and often furious enmity towards the EU; on the other, abject ambivalence.

I'll show what you I mean. Think of a prominent Remainer – an Umuna, perhaps, or a Soubry; a Clarke or even a Cable – and ask yourself how, in terms of raw passion and commitment, you would rank their pre-vote support for remaining in the EU. Most of us, even as we entered the polling booth, would have struggled to name a truly committed and passionate Remainer in the public eye. I know I would have done, and I've subsequently (and unexpectedly) become one. Now try the same exercise with prominent Leavers.

I wrote in the *TLS* shortly after the result that Remainers had turned up to a knife fight with battered boxing gloves and a borrowed copy of the Queensberry Rules (if nothing else, Brexit has at least allowed fans of tortuous analogies something of a field day). I'm not sure that was right. They weren't prepared for a fight at all. Charged with defending an obviously flawed organisation against claims that leaving it would deliver utopia, they had nothing in their arsenal save a status quo that many found profoundly unsatisfactory. If the debate stays simplistic and devoid of detail then it is surprisingly difficult to challenge someone who is offering an alternative to the status quo. You don't like the way things are? Well, vote for me and I promise I'll change things in ways no one else has ever promised. The louder the promise, the harder it is for voices pointing out its implausibility to be heard. Close to conclusive proof of this particular pudding resides, at the time of writing, in the White House.

I arrived at this conclusion partly because, like most people who have latterly concluded that membership of the European Union provided the United Kingdom with rather more benefits than problems, I didn't have particularly strong convictions about the issue until after the decision to leave it had been taken. The more I read and researched as part of the preparation for my show, the more I realised how sketchy my previous understanding had been. And when 'no deal' began to seem possible, speaking to people in the transport and haulage industries who understood precisely how catastrophic it would be left me as embarrassed as I was shocked.

People still on the other 'side', by contrast, have been persuaded for decades not only that the EU operated as some sort of enemy of British interests and even culture, but also that leaving would quickly and easily deliver myriad tangible benefits and expose the whole European project as doomed. But now reality has bitten, and we have learned more about the agents of persuasion, the breaking of electoral law and other tactics they employed, it has become easier to understand how such a fraudulent project could have proved so successful.

I still don't know what they think they won.

Chapter 3
LGBT

THERE'S A LINE IN Orwell's *Nineteen Eighty-Four* where his hero Winston Smith is describing the 'Two Minutes Hate' all residents of Oceania are compelled to conduct every day. It perfectly describes the sensibilities of right-wing tabloids and traditional radio phone-ins: 'And yet the rage that one felt was an abstract, undirected emotion which could be switched from one object to another like the flame of a blowlamp.'

It is not easy to simultaneously acknowledge the unerring accuracy of Orwell's insight – and so the appalling fickleness of those who are endlessly furious – while clinging to the belief that most people, given the chance, would prove to be fundamentally decent.

But it is not impossible. I realised quite early in my broadcasting career that even the most passionately held prejudices are vulnerable to the simplest of questions. And the fact that the target of the hate can move so quickly and so often is actually quite encouraging. It suggests that, for many, the hate is actually more about the hater than the hated, that its roots might not run too deep and so it might actually be possible to dig them up.

When I started the job in 2004, it was single mothers who bore the brunt of the blame for society's ills. Shortly afterwards, it was welfare claimants, and only relatively recently did Schrödinger's immigrant – the one who simultaneously steals 'our' jobs *and* claims unemployment benefit while leading a life of state-subsidised indolence – assume pole position on the starting grid of public contempt. Homosexuality, though, has always been in contention and I've never really understood why. As a white, heterosexual male, my bigotry buttons should surely be best pressed by people cast as somehow depriving me of something that is rightfully mine: our taxes, our housing, our jobs, our women, our status in society. None of these 'rights' are ever going to be threatened by a couple of blokes falling into bed together. Yet just five years before I was born in 1972, those blokes would have been committing a criminal offence and the idea that there is something fundamentally wrong with their very nature persists. Historically, few questions can light up a studio switchboard faster than ones inviting people to explain why they are disgusted or dismayed by a complete stranger's sexual preferences. But it is here that I derive the most confidence that it is possible to make people see things differently, however committed they might think they are to their original position.

The trick, as always, is to listen closely to what people say and then frame your next question to them accordingly. This might sound obvious, but you would be astonished to discover how many well-known journalists approach interviews with pre-prepared questions that they stick to regardless of the responses they receive. Nearly 20 years ago, as a cocky (and yet almost entirely scoop-free) newspaper showbusiness editor, I was wheeled into a BBC studio every month or so to act as a sort of sidekick to the 'proper' presenter, where I received a crash course in this practice. My role chiefly involved trying not to drink too much complimentary wine while waiting to chip in sporadically at the presenter's invitation. On this occasion, she was interviewing a proponent of so-called 'gay cure' therapies over the phone and I remember him using the phrase 'lifestyle choice' to describe homosexuality.

I was waiting for her to pounce on this arrant nonsense, but she didn't. She pressed on with another question, written in advance, about the prospect of criminalising such dangerous quackery. My discomfort must have been visible – I've always had the opposite of a poker face – because the producer suggested in my earphones that I should feel free to chip in. I didn't. The presenter was clearly less amenable to the notion than her producer and to do so would have involved unexpectedly interrupting her or her guest. Obviously, I'm less reticent now. But afterwards, I gave some thought to what sort of questions would have rubbished his opinion most effectively and it was the first time I wondered whether I might have what it takes to present debate-based current affairs programmes myself. It was a couple of years before I got the chance, but the experience meant I started to become more attuned to spotting the questions that I felt an interviewer should have asked. The habit persists, often to the annoyance of my family as I shout the questions I think an interviewer should be asking at the radio or television.

It seemed to me then, and I'm certain of it now, that the notion that sexuality involves any sort of choice is a remarkably odd position for anyone to take. That it is a claim so often made by homophobes – whether self-confessed, or camouflaged with religion – suggests that, for them, sexual preference is negotiable. It sounds a little trite to suggest that every homophobe must therefore be struggling with their own hated and hidden homosexuality, but why else are they so desperate to believe that being gay is a 'choice' – unless, of course, they are desperate to persuade themselves that *not* being gay is too?

I've had the following conversation at least a dozen times over the years. It never gets old or repetitive, despite being almost identical each time. I think this is because the certainty with which the caller begins is so complete that listening to it fall away is riveting. As the years have passed, I've tried to be more gentle with callers insisting that gay people don't really exist but I confess that there was a time when I could provoke spluttering fury from men down the phone by suggesting that what they really needed was a boyfriend. Perhaps I've matured. (Such callers have, so far, always been male. Female homophobes tend to appeal to scripture as opposed to the 'lifestyle choice' argument.) I'm going to do this one generically because it has happened so often and because it allows me to draw in every argument that people claiming sexuality is a 'lifestyle choice' have offered. However the conversation begins, I will always be leading the caller to this question.

James: So when did you choose to be straight?

Caller: What?

James: When did you choose to be straight?

Caller: I didn't choose to be straight. I was born straight.

James: But you literally just said that sexuality was a lifestyle choice. You said that gay people shouldn't be afforded full equality because they choose to be gay. You clearly think sexuality is a matter of choosing whom you fancy, so I'm wondering when you realised that you could go either way. When did you realise that you pretty much felt as excited about the prospect of sex with a man as you did about the prospect of sex with a woman and were going to have to choose which way to swing?

Caller: That's ridiculous. I have never felt excited about the prospect of sex with a man.

James: I agree that it sounds ridiculous but I'm just repeating your own logic back to you. Let's try again. How old are you?

Caller: Thirty four.

James: And you think you're straight?

Caller: I know I'm straight.

James: OK. Here's a theoretical 34-year-old gay man. Let's call him Bob. Bob knows he's gay. He's known since he was sexually conscious. He's never not been gay. But you are sure he's wrong and that he made a choice to be this way. He wants to know where you got that idea from, if not from your own experiences. Where would you get the idea that sexuality is something we choose, unless you have somehow tried to convince yourself that you can somehow choose to be straight despite, perhaps, having gay feelings?

Caller: I do not have gay feelings.

James: Bob does not have straight feelings. But the odd thing here is that he doesn't think that straight people chose to be straight any more than he chose to be gay. He's absolutely certain that all genuinely straight people have absolutely no choice about who or what they are sexually attracted to. He really wants to know where you got the idea that people can choose. And so do I, by the way.

Caller: It's against nature.

James: Not their nature. Anyway, flying thousands of feet in the air in a giant tin can is against nature, but you don't get your knickers in a twist about that. We just want to know, Bob and I, where you got the idea that you can choose your sexuality if it wasn't in some way from yourself. Did a gay person tell you that they had chosen to be gay but could easily have gone straight if the clubs and fashion had been better?

Caller: No.

James: So when did you choose to be straight?

Caller: I didn't choose to be straight.

James: Great. Nor did I. And Bob didn't choose to be gay. Do you get it now?

Of course, you never know whether they do or not, however they answer the question. But, more than any other subject until Brexit came along, it prompts people to get in touch to thank me for helping them change their minds. I mention this not to boast (well, not just to boast), but to highlight the difference a little gentle exploration of the foundations of their thinking can make to peoples' lives. Among the most memorable is an email I received from an electrician who described himself as a 'typical white van man' who'd never really thought about 'poofters' except as punchlines in jokes. Then his nephew came out as gay and, he said, he found himself repeating lines he'd heard on my show while trying to get his brother (the lad's father) to be less exercised and upset about it. He got in touch to thank me on behalf of all three of them. Emails like that stay with you in a way that even the most assiduous homophobic trolls can only dream of.

The people who believe that their religious faith demands a fascination with – and a profound aversion to – what complete strangers get up to in bed, present a rather different set of problems. I've spoken to Orthodox Jews who believe that God wants them to keep separate fridges for meat and dairy products; Jehovah's Witnesses who believe that blood transfusions are sinful and British Muslims who maintain that Western military interventions in countries they've never been near somehow justify acts of terror in their hometowns. While we're making a list, I'd add men from all three of these Abrahamic religions who think that women shouldn't be allowed to drive cars and the occasional woman who agrees with them. I give these examples to highlight the intractability of positions that outsiders find absurd but, in my experience, are just as likely to be built on shaky ground as political or secular moral opinions.

There are, of course, exceptions. Arguments so furiously bonkers that they will be impervious to both the scalpel and the sledgehammer approaches to questioning. Or interlocutors so completely blindsided by a point they hadn't heard before that the whole edifice of their convictions crumbles immediately. I was once commissioned to present a late-night debate show for Channel 4 which highlighted both of these possibilities. It was during a period of my career that saw me linked to more doomed pilots than the Japanese air force in the Second World War but, remarkably, this series was greenlit before we'd recorded a single second of footage and I was very excited about it, and not just because I really needed the money. The commissioning editor wanted something edgy, controversial and combative but was adamant that the debates mustn't be contrived. I've since encountered about a million commissioning editors with similar, equally daft, ambitions to manufacture rage while somehow staying serious but I was young, skint, under-employed and therefore determined to make this one work. We settled, with astonishing originality, on fox hunting and homosexuality as the subjects which would allow us to deliver entirely contrived studio rows that would hopefully strike the commissioning editor as being refreshingly uncontrived.

The first guest was a hunt saboteur with an impressive record of criminal convictions and a willingness to be filmed balaclava-clad in the way that sends a certain type of television producer weak at the knees. We had farmers, hunt supporters and even a kennelman ready to tear him to shreds like, well, hounds do a fox. But the first couple of questions would be mine. 'Why,' I wondered, 'do you focus so much attention on protecting foxes when every town in the country contains companies dedicated to killing all manner of other pests like rats and squirrels. They even go after urban foxes these days. Why don't you ever try to sabotage Rentokil?'

There was a pause which stretched to an uncomfortable length. When you hit a politician with a question they seem unable to answer, the feeling can be delicious, but in this context it could not have been worse. Eventually, he replied ponderously: 'Oh. I've never thought of it like that before. That's a really good point. I can't really answer it.'

I did my best but it's fair to say that we hadn't generated the studio fireworks that everyone involved in the project had presumed were a certainty.

Obviously, this was my fault. The question was too clever by half and, when you think about it, unlikely to elicit any sort of answer that could ignite the debate we wanted. So I approached the second topic, 'Is Homosexuality Wrong?' with an altogether simpler tactic.

'Why,' I asked a Northern Irish fire-and-brimstone preacher we'd flown to London especially, 'is homosexuality sinful?'

'It is not natural,' he bellowed immediately, 'to shove your fist up another man's anus.' To say that what followed was uncomfortable would be something of an understatement.

To the best of my knowledge, this became the only television debate programme to be commissioned without a pilot being made and then unceremoniously uncommissioned after the first episode had been recorded. Mercifully, it never saw the light of day. Not even on the blooper shows.

It is usually much easier – and much more fun – to do battle with the bigots who believe that their religious beliefs somehow entitle them to sit in judgment on other people's love lives. I saw it first hand at my Catholic monastic public school, where my sex education was undertaken by men in dresses who'd taken a vow of celibacy, and where some of my fellow pupils were tortured by the teachings that homosexual feelings were against God's will. It's probably not quite what Mum and Dad had in mind when they signed the cheques they could barely afford, but I came away with an impressive arsenal of scriptural weapons perfectly suited to dismantling the 'religious' homophobe.

I work from two simple premises. The first is to question why, of all the supposed instructions in the Bible, any Christian would choose to focus more on doctrines that are, at the very least, questionable interpretations of scripture than, for example, the unequivocal condemnation of, say, adultery in the Ten Commandments, or the description of shellfish as an 'abomination' in the book of Leviticus. The second, very simply, is to focus on what Jesus actually said. This isn't the place to examine my own relationship with religion, which is complicated to say the least. Suffice to say that a lifetime of Catholic indoctrination has left me convinced that Jesus Christ, as reported in the Gospels, is among the most powerful moral philosophers of all time.

David, a 'lay preacher', rang me after the then leader of the Liberal Democrats, Tim Farron, had described gay sex as a sin. The challenges laid down that morning were to support Farron by citing words that Jesus had said and/or to explain why some 'religious' types seem so obsessed with homosexuality. I should probably warn you that this one went 'viral' under the headline: 'James O'Brien Asks Caller Same Question On Jesus's Comments on Gay People 27 TIMES'. So I've tried to edit it down a bit.

David: The Bible's quite clear with regards to homosexuality and what is a sin and what isn't a sin.

James: Which bit of the Bible?

David: The Old and New Testament. I'll get into that further down the line.

James: No. Let's do it now, because we should get it out of the way early. The New Testament contains a couple of quotes from St Paul and an interpretation of the word 'sodomite' ... but just remind me what Jesus actually said.

David: I'm trying to do that.

James: Go on then.

David: What you have to understand about the Bible, James, is that it's God-inspired, also many, many people contributed to the Bible so Paul is relevant. He wrote most of the New Testament, so if you're trying to excuse Paul's teachings you have to excuse the whole Bible. You can't cherry-pick the things you like and the things you don't like. So Paul—

James: So you're not going to tell me what Jesus said?

David: I will if you let me get a word in.

James: Here is the question. What did Jesus say about homosexuality? David will now answer that question directly.

[Pause]

David: In First Corinthians. In the God-inspired Bible in First Corinthians, Paul wrote—'

James: First Corinthians is a letter that St Paul wrote. What did Jesus say, in the Gospels, about homosexuality?

David: Are you refuting the Bible then? So you can't be a Christian then.

James: It's a simple question. What did Jesus say? You can say 'Nothing, James' because that's the true answer, or you can carry on blustering.

David: I'm not carrying on blustering, James.

James: Good. So what did Jesus say about homosexuality?

David: OK. So when Paul spoke he was speaking through Paul, was he not? God, Jesus, was speaking through Paul. [sic]

James: Listen. I will give you all the time you need to answer the question that I am actually asking you. Either you repeat the words that Jesus said about homosexuality, or you say that he didn't say anything. What are you going to choose? Did he say anything and, if so, what are the words?

David: That's not the right question, James.

James: OK. So let's go back to the other question we started with. Why do some religious types – no, let's talk about you. Why do you care so much about gay people?

David: You're putting words in my mouth. I didn't say I cared so much about gay people.

James: Well, you phoned up on an issue about gay people and religion. You've identified yourself as religious so now I want to know why you care about the other bit of the debate, which is gayness.

David: If you let me get a word out, James. It's called a conversation. It's supposed to be a two-way street.

James: David, mate, you can say this all you want. The question you have singularly declined to answer is 'What did Jesus say about homosexuality?' and we both know the reason why you're not answering that question is because he said diddly squat. So now I'm asking why you think your religion cares so much about homosexuality. Now conversation is a two-way street, but it's not an exercise in me asking you a question and you answering a completely different one.

David: I don't think religion cares so much about homosexuality. It's people like you that discuss it all the time. The Bible is clear about what is sinful and what is not sinful. The Bible doesn't care so much about homosexuality.

James: OK. So one more time, David my brother. What did Jesus say about homosexuality?

David: I've already answered that question.

James: I don't remember that. What did Jesus say about homosexuality? How did you answer that question? Go ...

David: If you let me speak. When Paul spoke in the New Testament it was God who was speaking through him. So

Jesus might not have ... You're referring to Jesus's words in there when it's quoted in the Bible, but there's other people in the Bible who wrote letters and scriptures in the Bible that are God-inspired, so it was God who spoke through Paul when he wrote that.

James: What did Jesus say about homosexuality, David?

David: So you don't like the answer that I've given you. You just don't like it. Let me write that down.

James: What did Jesus say about homosexuality, David?

David: I've given you the answer.

James: So what were the words that Jesus said? Quoting Jesus, in the gospels, he said ...

David: It's unfortunate, James, that you don't like the answer, but that's the answer.

James: What did he say, David? Just give me the quote. Just one line. You don't need chapter and verse. What did Jesus say about homosexuality?

David: 'First Corinthians Six when Jesus spoke to Paul—

James: That's a letter St Paul wrote. What did Jesus say?

David: I already told you, James.

James [singing in a Gospel music style]: What did Jesus say?

David: I already told you. Jesus spoke through Paul in First Corinthians—

James [still singing]: But what did Jesus say?

David: I just don't understand where you're coming from.

James [singing]: What did Jesus say, about people who are gay?

David: I told you. First Corinthians—

James: That's a letter written by someone who never met Jesus. What did Jesus say?

And on we could have gone until, presumably, Judgment Day. If we hadn't already been very late for the travel news.

The Old Testament provides, if anything, even more ammunition for attacks on homophobia. As ever, it begins with the meaning of words. In this case: abomination. Specifically, Leviticus 18:22 where it is written 'You shall not lie with a male as with a woman; it is an abomination.' Let's forget for now the scholarship that attempts, with mixed success, to interpret this as a criticism of promiscuity, adultery and idolatry and focus instead on just how seriously 'Christians' want to take Levitican instruction.

George in Anstruther is a phone-in radio staple: a man so enraged by homosexuality that you occasionally wonder whether there is something of the performance to his contributions. He is a rhetorical cousin of the cleric from that Channel 4 pilot with the anal fisting obsession and, as with David, he thinks the Bible somehow justifies his position.

George: It is an abomination for a man to lie with a man as he does with a woman.

James: How do you feel about lobsters?

George: What?

James: Lobsters. I know Anstruther quite well. Lovely part of the world. Great fish and chips and a thriving seafood trade up there in Fife. How do you feel about lobsters?

George: I don't think I've ever had lobster.

James: Prawns, then? Or scallops? Or a lovely crab? I only ask because Leviticus is pretty explicit on the subject. Chapter 11, verses 10 to 12. 'And all that have not fins and scales in the seas, and in the rivers, of all that move in the waters, and of any living thing which is in the waters, they shall be an abomination unto you. They shall be even an abomination unto you; ye shall not eat of their flesh, but ye shall have their carcasses in abomination. Whatsoever hath no fins nor scales in the waters, that shall be an abomination unto you.' On a scale of one to ten, George, how much outrage do your religious beliefs demand that you direct at people who eat prawns?

George: That's ridiculous.

James: I know. So now we need to wonder why you choose to get so exercised about gay people getting it on while remaining so relaxed about people munching their way through a big plate of *fruits de mer*. By your own rationale, surely they're deserving of equal condemnation. Leviticus even uses the same word, George.

George: The Bible is clear that it is sinful for a man to lie with another man. You can fanny about all you like, but a sin is a sin.

James: What are you wearing, George?

George: What?

James: What are you wearing? Don't worry, I'm not initiating phone sex.

George: I don't see that it's any of your business.

James: Indulge me, George, or just pretend. Do you, for example, own a Harris Tweed jacket?

George: What if I do?

James: 'Well, according to Leviticus 19:19, you're violating God's law if you ever wear it. You are committing a sin comparable, according to Leviticus, to lying with a man as with a woman. It's stated pretty clearly that you're not allowed to wear garments made of two different kinds of thread.

Conversations like this, replete with Biblical citations, can also include the sinfulness of approaching an altar if you need contact lenses, playing football with a pigskin ball, getting a haircut or working on the Sabbath, the latter being punishable by death by stoning no less. You can also use the Old Testament to justify selling your daughter into slavery and keeping slaves of your own, as long as they have been purchased from neighbouring nations.

You may already be familiar with some of this. In an October 2000 episode of the White House drama *The West Wing*, President Bartlet, played by Martin Sheen, uses such knowledge to completely destroy the Biblical justifications for homophobia put forward by, appropriately enough, a right-wing talk-show host. His brilliant speech was based upon a letter sent to a real-life American one, Laura Schlessinger, that subsequently went viral on the internet. A listener sent me the 'Dr Laura' letter early on in my radio career and I have it to hand whenever callers like George reach for the Book of Leviticus. And the ease with which you can find everything you need to debunk such bigotry these days makes me wonder whether people like him, and to a lesser extent David, would rather live with all that ignorant fury than with an altogether more peaceful truth.

It also makes me wonder about the motivation behind legislation like Section 28 of the Local Government Act 1988. Introduced by Margaret Thatcher and championed by the likes of Norman Tebbit, it stated that local authorities 'shall not intentionally promote homosexuality or publish material with the intention of promoting homosexuality' or 'promote the teaching in a mainstream school of the acceptability of homosexuality as a pretended family relationship'.

The fear, which doesn't seem dissimilar to the one expressed by my brigade of 'lifestyle choice' callers, is clearly that portraying homosexuality as normal might somehow persuade previously heterosexual people to jump into bed with the nearest willing member of the same sex. As this, for reasons that are never properly explained, would be a matter of unutterable calamity.

Of all the non-news issues I've puzzled over on air over the years, this is probably the one that upsets me the most. In 2014, 14 years after Section 28 was consigned to the dustbin of history, a survey found 52 per cent of young LGBT people had self-harmed, compared to 25 per cent of heterosexual non-trans young people.* Meanwhile, 44 per cent of young LGBT people had considered suicide, compared to 26 per cent of heterosexual non-trans young people. Our young people are still harming and killing themselves on a disproportionate scale and corners of our media and political establishments are still reluctant to teach children that homosexuality is unremarkable and perfectly normal.

Of course, they don't all do it because they are terrified of their own secret sexuality, or worried they might somehow 'catch' homosexuality. Some of them do it because, as we have established previously with other issues, there is

---

* 'Youth Chances' survey, January 2014. Led by the homosexual advocacy group Metro and funded by the Big Lottery Research Fund.

money to be made by poisoning the well of public discourse, turning neighbours, family members and colleagues against each other and flogging the idea that just to be different is somehow to be wrong.

Disgraced former *Sun* editor Kelvin MacKenzie put it best in the early eighties, when he was quoted as saying:

> *You just don't understand the readers, do you, eh? He's the bloke you see in the pub, a right old fascist, wants to send the wogs back, buy his poxy council house, he's afraid of the unions, afraid of the Russians, hates the queers and the weirdos and drug dealers. He doesn't want to hear about that stuff (serious news).*[*]

Like Orwell, MacKenzie understood that the focus of the rage can move around 'like a blowlamp'. Unlike Orwell, editors, owners and columnists like MacKenzie see it as a fantastic opportunity. In recent years, with the dread forces of 'political correctness' successfully dousing most of the flames of blatant homophobia, the blowlamp has instead settled on trans people, particularly trans women, and, for me at least, this has provided a sometimes uncomfortable education.

---

[*] *Stick It Up Your Punter: the Rise and Fall of the Sun* by Peter Chippindale & Chris Horrie, Heinemann, 1990.

In short, every time I speak to a trans woman I come away convinced that they deserve to be treated like someone born with female genitals, even if they are in possession of a penis. And every time a non-trans woman explains to me that she feels frightened by the prospect of a predatory male pretending to be a trans woman in order to gain access to restricted female spaces, I feel the pendulum of my opinion swinging in their support. I'm not exaggerating: in the space of four calls to the programme, I can quite easily change my mind three times. But I think this is healthy. Despite the title of this book, it is refreshing, in an age of increasingly reductionist and binary debate, to recognise the importance of sometimes saying the three most undervalued words in the English language: I don't know.

'Self-identification', the legal process by which a biological male can assume every single right currently enjoyed by biological females simply by stating that s/he *is* a woman, is clearly problematic. There are a number of reasons why I lean toward supporting it, though. First, the examples of Ireland and elsewhere suggest that many of the fears expressed by people who don't want it to make its way onto the statute book in the UK are largely unfounded. Secondly, I'd point also to the fact that the patron saint of twenty-first-century bigotry, Donald Trump, reached very early for trans people (in the military) as an 'acceptable' target for the type of discrimination that has thankfully been rooted out of many other areas of public life. This, to me, suggests, but doesn't prove, that trans women are just the latest in a long line of people it is easy to 'other' and use to spook people who are frightened of change. The language of the debates is so telling: as with homosexuality 30 years ago, rhetoric revolves around the 'fear' that normalising trans women might somehow persuade boys to whom the idea would never have otherwise occurred to have their genitals surgically removed. This old idea of contagion is never far from the surface.

But, ultimately, and with the caveat that I am still not comfortable telling women that they have to throw open their changing rooms and toilets to all biologically male people who self-identify as female, I try to find the position that will minimise the likelihood of there being another Lucy Meadows.

In December 2012, a Welsh primary school sent its pupils home for the holidays with a letter about changes that would be in place at the beginning of the next term. Mrs Metcalfe, for example, was leaving for a new position in Spain. Mrs Kelly was set to reduce her hours and Mr Caton would be joining Mrs Mulcock as a year two teacher. Mr Upton, the parents learned, 'has recently made a significant change in his life and will be transitioning to live as a woman. After the Christmas break, she will return to work as Miss Meadows.'

According to Lucy's former wife, Ruth Smith, one parent complained about the news because his child was 'confused' and started a petition to protest. He also spoke to the local press and by doing so, we must presume unintentionally, set in motion a tragic chain of events.

On 20 December, the *Daily Mail* columnist Richard Littlejohn wrote an article headlined 'He's not only in the wrong body … he's in the wrong job.' The deliberate mis-gendering aside, he wrote with characteristic crassness of the 'devastating effect' Lucy's change in gender would have upon her pupils.

'Why,' he asked, 'should they be forced to deal with the news that a male teacher they have always known as Mr Upton will henceforth be a woman called Miss Meadows?' Littlejohn did not reveal whether his concern was based on more than the confusion of a single child and his parent's petition. He certainly did not mention the many expressions of support and encouragement that Miss Meadows had received from other parents, pupils and colleagues.

Two and a half months later, she was dead. Two and a half months after Lucy's suicide, the coroner at her inquest accused the *Daily Mail* of 'ridicule and humiliation' and a 'character assassination' of 32-year-old Lucy.

As he closed the inquest, Michael Singleton, coroner for Blackburn, Hyndburn and Rossendale, turned to the reporters present and said:

And to you the press, I say shame, shame on all of you. Lucy Meadows was not somebody who had thrust herself into the public limelight. She was not a celebrity. She had done nothing wrong. Her only crime was to be different. Not by choice but by some trick of nature. And yet the press saw fit to treat her in the way that they did.

The Press Complaints Commission carried out an investigation and on 11 March 2013 the *Daily Mail* offered to take down Littlejohn's article from the paper's website, as well as a photograph of Meadows's wedding to Smith in February 2009. But, of course, as Ruth later wrote: 'Once online, always online. Our private moment, for me and my family, put out there.'

Singleton was, to say the least, unimpressed by the *Daily Mail*'s gesture. 'Having carried out what can only be described as a character assassination,' he said, 'having sought to ridicule and humiliate Lucy Meadows and bring into question her right to pursue her career as a teacher, the *Daily Mail*'s response was to offer to remove the article from the website.'

I don't know whether self-identification is as wholly innocuous as its most ardent defenders insist. I don't know whether the risk of predatory males pretending to be trans women in order to commit sexual assaults and rapes is as acute as others contend. I certainly don't know at what age medical intervention should be permitted. After having a couple of on-air debates on the subject, I don't even know whether I should still be allowed to accompany my young daughters into the fitting rooms at Gap when we're shopping without their mum.

But I do know that 'journalism' like Littlejohn's is as dangerous as it is despicable and that, for me, the 'right' side of this particular argument will always involve being on the opposite side to him and his ilk. At the time of writing, Richard Littlejohn reportedly remains the highest paid newspaper columnist in the country.

Chapter 4
POLITICAL CORRECTNESS

THE LATE BRITISH SATIRIST and genius Peter Cook famously explained that his 1960s Soho nightclub, The Establishment, was modelled on 'those wonderful Berlin cabarets which did so much to stop the rise of Hitler and prevent the outbreak of the Second World War.'

Thirty years later, the puppeteer satirists responsible for the seminal *Spitting Image* TV show had their grotesque latex puppets, which depicted various politicians, screech the phrase 'It's political correctness gone mad!' in response to any suggestion that people might moderate their language, behaviour or manner to avoid causing unnecessary offence to others. Their attempt to defuse the phrase has proved as successful as those Berlin cabarets.

It's fascinating to see people who are offended by pretty much everything – gay people getting married; students removing poems or portraits of politicians from college walls; toilets that anyone can use; councils putting up fairy lights to mark religious festivals – insist that *they* are the implacable enemies of people who take unnecessary offence at the world around them. I could, on any given day, fill the switchboard six times over with callers primed to rail furiously against 'snow-flakes' and 'social justice warriors' who take offence too easily. Not a single one of them would be alive to the irony that they were taking violent offence at largely innocuous actions which they wouldn't be remotely aware of if the media wasn't committed to keeping them furiously offended on a daily basis.

It would be funny if it hadn't led, inevitably but again not necessarily intentionally, to people in public life today making the absurd claim that their free speech has been stifled. I can assure you, as my callers prove daily on national radio, that you can say pretty much whatever you want about pretty much anything you please in modern Britain. But millions remain perversely convinced that they can't, because of 'political correctness'. It's a short hop from here, of course, to arguing that anyone attempting to question or criticise 'free speech' is an agent of 'political correctness' and, hey presto, the ludicrous conclusion that 'liberals are the new fascists' becomes a credo for the professionally offended and the permanently outraged.

When were you last offended on somebody else's behalf? This morning I saw a Facebook post in which the black politician Diane Abbott's face had been superimposed onto the body of a morbidly obese woman in an ill-fitting superhero bikini-style costume. The 'punchline' was 'Beware of Blunder Woman' and I took a moment to ponder both why I felt the person responsible, an Irish newspaper journalist in his early sixties, had crossed a line, and precisely where my own moral compass had drawn that line.

Would I have felt the same if the target of the 'joke' had been white? On reflection, yes. Abbott receives industrial amounts of racist and misogynistic abuse every single day, but here it was the overt sexualisation of the image and, the judgment of her perceived ugliness that offended me. Would I have felt the same if the target had been a man? No. As a straight man, my life is effectively free from any threat of sexual violence. I had an ugly eye infection a couple of years ago which prompted a glut of 'hilarious' fourth-rate photoshopping from internet trolls, but nothing like an image designed to render a woman simultaneously sexual, vulnerable and unattractive.

What if somebody picked me up now on the use of the word 'superhero' here? There are, I'm sure, people who strongly believe that I should have said 'superheroine' or 'superperson' and while I currently think they're wrong, my mind remains open and I'd be happy to discuss it. Hoary old chestnuts of linguistic 'political correctness' usually focus on words like 'chairmen' and 'blackboards'. Telling people that there is something implicitly offensive about words they've used without a second thought for decades is more fraught than many realise. It doesn't make you reactionary or even prejudiced to bridle at being told, usually by a much younger person, that you've spent years using words you don't understand. But you can have a conversation, arrive at a compromise, agree to disagree. That we so often fail to do so speaks of intransigence on both sides.

This, though, is the ultimate aim of the war against 'political correctness'. Its foot soldiers seek to silence opinions they find discomforting and to arrest social developments they consider threatening to a status quo that has delivered undeserved privilege to straight, white men like me for centuries. And they do it while claiming to be somehow on the side of tolerance and freedoms, claiming that 'you can't give offence, you can only take it', without realising that they spend their lives being offended by just about everything.

Some of this escalating of tensions is deliberate. For example, pretending not to understand that the Black Lives Matter movement seeks a society where black lives matter to law enforcement officers *as much as* white lives do. Some of it is accidental, such as when stories that appear to support the narrative of censorship and suppression and whatever is meant by 'cultural Marxism' achieve currency without being properly examined or understood.

It is not a pleasant experience for these foot soldiers to have their ideas about 'political correctness' examined in the light. But it is remarkable how rarely the generals – the columnists and demagogues – are asked to explain theirs. For theirs is a narrative of victimhood; highly-paid beneficiaries of a profoundly unfair system whose entire careers are built upon persuading less privileged people that they are somehow under siege, or losing their 'identity'. It is a lucrative business and those who buy into this narrative rarely realise how comprehensively they have been duped, because the daft conclusions they've been led to are so rarely properly scrutinised. So it is that the scantest examination can leave them horribly exposed.

Marian in Sutton Coldfield, for example, was convinced that Union Flags were routinely removed from municipal buildings in order to avoid offending Muslims. It's easy to laugh but this remains a very widely held belief and, if it were true, it would not be unreasonable to be offended, or even outraged. After a few years in the job I had heard this argument more than a few times and so took it upon myself to find out whether it contained any kernel of truth. Marian was the first caller to enjoy the fruits of my research.

James: I've looked into this, Marian, and I'm pretty sure that what you're describing has only happened once, with a flag of St George rather than a Union Jack, and the council reversed the decision after a few days when it emerged that nobody had complained about the flag being flown in the first place.

Marian: Rubbish, James. I know you're only trying to calm me down but it happens all the time. When's the last time you saw a Union Jack flying outside a town hall?'

James: I don't know, to be honest I haven't looked, but that's not quite the same thing as proving that flags have been taken down for fear of offending Muslims, is it? And why would the Union Jack be offensive to Muslims anyway?

> **Marian:** I don't know. Ask them.
>
> **James:** I have. It isn't. There was a case in Somerset a couple of years ago where a councillor, who wasn't a Muslim, reckoned that the Cross of St George's associations with the Crusades might be offensive to Muslims and it got reported as a shining example of political correctness gone mad. But do you want to know what really happened?

I'm not sure what the ethical position is on a presenter using the internet to conduct live research into a caller's position, but I'm generally comfortable with it. On this occasion, I knew both what I was looking for and what I would find. It might seem a bit unfair but Marian could have done it herself in moments and I can't search for details like names and dates unless I'm already aware of a story's existence. The details make my refutations much more compelling and, of course, if a caller insists that something demonstrably untrue is true – not because they're dishonest or bigoted but because they're being fed this rubbish by others on a daily basis – it seems to me to be respectful to provide them with as much evidence as possible.

> **Marian:** You're going to tell me anyway.
>
> **James:** It was in a little town in Somerset called Radstock, population 5,600, of whom 16 were reckoned to be Muslim. They were having a discussion about what new flag to buy after

their flagpole had been repaired and a Labour councillor argued that they should avoid flying the flag of St George for 20 years because its links with the Crusades might offend Muslims, but more so because it had been hijacked in recent years by the far right. Is this ringing any bells?

Marian: Did they buy the flag?

James: No. The council voted not to.

Marian: Well, then.

James: They voted to buy a Union Flag instead because, and this is quite important I think, they only had one flagpole. But the newspapers got hold of the story, twisted it completely, and used the manipulated facts to convince decent people like you that national traditions are somehow being threatened by political correctness gone mad.

Marian: You're patronising me now.

James: I don't think I am. I'm thinking that when you're actually given the full story you'll change your position and that will be one less thing to be cross about. Surely the real patronising has been done by people who think they can sell you a bunch of lies and half-truths without you noticing?

Marian: But they didn't buy the flag of St George. And it was because Muslims didn't want them to.

James: No. They didn't buy the flag of St George because they only had one flagpole and felt that the Union Flag would be a better bet than a specifically English one. The council chair actually explained this in some of the original reports, albeit far down the story and under headlines designed to make you think exactly what you ended up thinking. I've got the quote here: 'The statement made by one councillor regarding the St George's flag was not really taken into consideration.' But do you know what a spokesman for the Bristol Muslim Cultural Society said at the time? Trust me, you'll like this.

Marian: What?

James: He said: 'I think they are going a bit far here. It is political correctness going a bit too far.' The Muslim Council of Britain went even further. They said: 'St George needs to take his rightful place as a national symbol of inclusivity rather than a symbol of hatred.'

Marian: Well, why did they say that the flag was taken down after complaints from Muslims?

James: They didn't. The headline on top of the story I'm reading now says, 'Council vetoes flag of St George after concerns raised about links To Crusades'. Do you see? They've taken the facts – and this is my dad's old paper so it pains me to point it out – and packaged them up in a way that's deliberately and cynically designed to make you think that Muslims demanded the flag be somehow taken down. It didn't even exist. It was only ever a theoretical flag, subject to theoretical complaints from theoretical Muslims which, according to the actual leader of the actual council, weren't even taken into account during the decision-making process. Do you want to know what happened next?

Marian: I do, actually, yes.

James: The councillor who made the original comments, which we now know didn't inform the decision-making process, was offered police protection after receiving death threats. She issued a grovelling apology and the council voted the following week to buy a St George's flag after all, which they'll be able to fly whenever they're not flying the Union Flag.

Marian: You must drive your wife mad, you're such a know-it-all.

James: I'm not going to argue with that, Marian, but I did use Google. Can we agree now that Muslims don't get Union Jacks taken down from council buildings?

Marian: Yes. Yes we can.

I will be a bit patronising now. It often seems as if this phrase 'political correctness' excuses people from thinking for themselves. It really did pain me that the story above was lifted from the pages of the *Daily Telegraph* because, perhaps naively, I don't think that respectable newspapers engaged in this sort of propaganda when I was young and my dad was writing for them. He often talked about the point in his career when the *Sun* newspaper, not long after it was bought by Rupert Murdoch, started reporting on stories in a way that all the other journalists working on the same story didn't recognise. Where once the 'press pack' would be filing variations on the same theme, Murdoch's *Sun* seemed to be reporting a different reality. Of course, that reality proved commercially a lot more popular than the one being dutifully described by all the other newspapers. The 50 years since Murdoch vowed never to print 'upmarket shit' in his paper have seen most of the right-wing newspapers move incrementally closer to the *Sun*'s triumphant business model of selling tickets for a ghost train in full knowledge that ghosts don't exist.

And where 'mainstream media' leads, social media follows, with even less policing of facts. Consider this bleakly simple press release that Coventry City Council were compelled to issue in July 2017, and then consider how few of the people who saw the original nonsense pop up in their Facebook feeds will have subsequently been made aware of the truth. It is not their fault they have been misled any more than it was Marian's, but it seems disingenuous to dismiss 'fake news' on the internet when so much of it apes the antics of the country's biggest newspapers.

We've been made aware of a story circulating on Facebook about the Council that isn't true. The post claims that the Council sent a bailiff to a Coventry address because a Union Jack flag was displayed. This is not true. While we cannot discuss the specific reasons for a debt recovery, we

> *can categorically say the debt being recovered here is not connected to a fine for displaying a Union Jack as has been claimed on social media.*

There are also stories about council tenants being ordered to take down flags but, without exception, I have found these to be either confected or simply a result of regulations regarding any form of decoration, particularly in communal areas. A flat near me in London has had a sad, nylon flag of St George dangling from its balcony since the 2014 football World Cup. It currently resembles a manky, oversized grey dishcloth. In the right hands, of course, any request that the resident remove it could and no doubt would be cast as yet another example of 'political correctness gone mad'.

More recently, a dozen or so students decided to mount a protest at a London cafe themed around the wartime prime minister, Winston Churchill. They defaced a mural dedicated to him with the words 'Imperialist Scum' and argued that the cafe made light of colonial injustices. Immense outrage followed. Newspapers with a combined readership approaching ten million reported the story furiously, columnists wrote feverish opinion pieces, readers wrote impassioned comments of condemnation. None of them stopped to wonder, though, who was really making a bigger display of taking offence: the handful of (for my money quite silly) protesting students, or the millions of people around the word successfully encouraged to be profoundly offended by them. This is real Emperor's New Clothes territory for me. It sometimes seems that half the country is furiously convinced that so-called 'snowflakes' are too easily offended while they literally splutter with rage at a primary school's toilet policy, a student union's decision not to have a Rudyard Kipling poem on their wall or a non-existent flag removal.

Perhaps the most infamous example of all this is 'Winterval'. It has since been overshadowed, but for a significant period of time in the first decade of the millennium it was held up, almost entirely without challenge, as irrefutable evidence that 'pandering to minorities' was somehow 'undermining our culture'. The cultural event being threatened in this case was Christmas, that most Anglo-Saxon of festivals whereby the birth of a Jewish baby in a Middle Eastern stable two thousand years ago is commemorated.

Andrew in Erith was far from alone when he insisted that you 'weren't even allowed to celebrate Christmas any more'.

James: Where can't you celebrate it, mate?

Andrew: Anywhere.

James: Really? Have they been round your house? Told you to take down your tree? Confiscated your tinsel? Made a bonfire of holly and ivy?

Andrew: No. Anywhere in public.

James: What, you mean like in a church or a town square or a school?

Andrew: Yeah. You can't celebrate it in case it offends other people.

James: Andrew, are you aware of anyone, anywhere in this country being told that they can't celebrate Christmas?

Andrew: Yes, James, that's what I'm telling you. You have to call it Winterval now.

James: In Erith?

Andrew: Everywhere.

James: Right. Here's the thing. For a couple of years before the millennium, Birmingham City Council tried to save a few quid by leaving the street lights up and tying together loads of different things under the title Winterval, short for winter festival.

Andrew: Exactly. So you couldn't call it Christmas anymore.

James: You could call *Christmas* Christmas, Andrew. It was the biggest bit of Winterval, but the bloke in charge of arranging municipal events, bless him, thought it would make life easier and cheaper if they treated it like a season of celebration. Do you know what else it included?

Andrew: No.

James: Right. This is pretty much straight from Wikipedia. The Council's head of events at the time was a chap called Chubb. According to him, among other things, Winterval covered Diwali, the Hindu Festival of Lights, which was in October, and the Christmas lights switch-on, which was obviously a few weeks later. It also covered the BBC's Children in Need, a candlelight service at a stately home in the city, Chinese New Year and New Year's Eve. It was a well-meaning attempt by a council employee to create a festival season that would bring business to Birmingham for a much longer period than just Christmas. In his own words: 'a season that included theatre shows, an open-air ice-rink, the Frankfurt open-air Christmas market and the Christmas season retail offer. Christmas – *called Christmas!* – and its celebration lay at the heart of Winterval. The front cover of the promotion brochure used the word 'Christmas' three times and featured a photograph of the city's official Christmas tree. Each of its six pages featured the word 'Christmas' in text or images. Did any of this happen in Erith, Andrew?

Andrew: That's not the point. Why can't you just call it Christmas? That's what we mean about political correctness.

James: Why would you want to call Chinese New Year 'Christmas', mate?

Andrew: What?

James: Why would you want to call Chinese New Year 'Christmas', or Children In Need or the Hindu Festival of Light?

Andrew: Why are we even celebrating them?

James: We're not. Well, you're not and nobody's telling you to. You're just celebrating Christmas while simultaneously claiming that you somehow can't. By the next year, Winterval included Guy Fawkes, Halloween, the Muslim festival of Eid and the Jewish festival of Hanukkah. Do you see why it was quite a good idea, at least in principle, to try to sell Birmingham as a kind of festival city but that they needed a name that could cover all the festivals?

Andrew: Not really, no. I just want to celebrate Christmas as Christmas. A Christian festival.

James: In Birmingham in 1997 or in Erith now?

Andrew: What do you mean?

James: Well if you wanted to celebrate it in Brum in 1997, here's the council's description of what was going on: 'There was a banner saying Merry Christmas across the front of the council house, Christmas lights, Christmas trees in the main civic squares, regular carol-singing sessions by school choirs and the Lord Mayor sent a Christmas card with a traditional Christmas scene wishing everyone a Merry Christmas.' You have to tell me now how you've been prevented from doing any of this, or even calling Christmas Christmas, in Erith in 2010.

Obviously, Andrew couldn't really come back from a barrage of evidence which pops up pretty much immediately if you just google 'Winterval'. I'm often asked how I have all this stuff at my fingertips but, while I have a bit of a magpie memory, most of it is at everybody else's fingertips too. Every columnist, talk-show host, politician or barrack room lawyer who has talked of 'Winterval' in the intervening years could have availed themselves of the real facts in a matter of seconds. In light of this, it is somewhat telling that the *Daily Mail* felt compelled to issue the following correction in 2011: 'Winterval was the collective name for a season of public events, both religious and secular, which took place in Birmingham in 1997 and 1998. We are happy to make clear that Winterval did not rename or replace Christmas.'

Unsurprisingly, the whole idea was dropped after just two years and I don't know what happened to its instigator, the Council's Head of Events Mike Chubb. I hope he flourished. His unwitting legacy remains one of the most stark examples of how almost all claims that 'political correctness has gone mad' invariably turn out to be based on hokum and hot air. The intervening years, alas, have done nothing to dilute the potency of the phrase. Neither have they brought us any closer to understanding precisely what people mean when they employ it. Largely, as usual, because those people hardly ever get asked.

Geoff in Macclesfield had a personal interest in the decision by the department store John Lewis to sell 'gender neutral' clothes for children. He runs his own clothing company and found the decision to eschew 'girls' and 'boys' labels outrageous.

Geoff: What's wrong with just having 'boys' and 'girls'? I mean, I don't understand why they would want to bow to political correctness.

James: Why do you think it's political correctness? What do you mean by that phrase?

Geoff: We hear that all the time now.

James: I know, but no one can ever tell me what it means. What do you think it means?

Geoff: Political correctness?

James: Yes. What does it mean?

Geoff: It means trying to say or do something that doesn't offend anybody at all.

James: But loads of people like you are really offended by this.

Geoff: They are. That's right.

James: So it doesn't mean that, does it?

Geoff: It does mean that, but you're always going to offend someone. There will always be someone who, sadly, doesn't agree with the rest.

James: So it's bad to try not to be offensive?

Geoff: No. You should try not to be offensive.

James: But that's political correctness.

Geoff: You can't please all of the people all of the time.

James: I know that, but your definition of political correctness was trying not to offend people. So that's either a good thing

HOW TO BE RIGHT

or a bad thing. It can't be both. Did you maybe mean trying *too hard* not to be offensive?'

Geoff: Yes. Trying too hard.

James: So how hard should we try?

Geoff: As hard as is reasonable.

James: And who decides what's reasonable?

Geoff : [Laughs] Very good. But that's just playing with words.

James: No, hang on mate. Political and correctness are words that you were playing with and I'm just trying to work out what you mean by them.

Geoff: Fair comment.

James: It's not a comment, it's a question. What do you mean when you say we shouldn't try so hard not to offend? The logical conclusion might be that you think we should all try a bit harder to be offensive. All these people going around trying to minimise insult and offence are ridiculous. We should be a lot more insulting and offensive. Is that it?

Geoff: To go back to your question of who decides, I guess whoever owns the business decides and that's John Lewis and that's fine.

James: But why would you use that phrase, though? It's the one that pops up in all of the most, forgive me, thoughtless contributions to social media and comments sections. Why is it political correctness? Why do you care how kids' clothes are labelled?

There's a long pause here. In my experience, the longer the pause, the more honest the caller.

Geoff: I guess I don't really care. I'm just thinking about how it would affect me and my business if I had to do it. If I was forced to do it.

James: OK. So it's the idea that, on the horizon, it could become somehow illegal to say that *that's* for boys and *that's* for girls?

Geoff: Yes.

James: OK. And to indulge that slightly fanciful theory for a moment, what's the worst that could happen if that did occur?

Geoff: You get guidance from the government that you cannot use those words.

James: But even then, what's the worst that could happen? In the context of your life and business people are still going to need clothes. They're going to need exactly the same number of garments for exactly the same number of people. It's just the words that would change. What's the worst thing that would happen in your world, if you were somehow told that you now had to sell clothes for people instead of for men and women. And even, if you want to get physiological about it, these are the clothes for people with boobs and these are the ones for people who haven't got boobs.

Geoff: Well, that really is the worst that could happen, I suppose. We would just go to female fit and male fit. It wouldn't be the end of the world.

James: Is it even an issue, Geoff, when you really stop to think about it? Is it really even an issue? When you engage your brain and set aside echoes of ludicrous right-wing vocabulary like 'political correctness', it doesn't matter a jot.

Geoff: Then why do it in the first place?

James: Because it matters to the young people that this will benefit. The ones you think we should be trying harder to offend.

Geoff: But who does that affect?

James: Children. Children who don't want to be told that there's something somehow wrong with them if they're drawn naturally to certain clothes.

Geoff: You're not being told there's anything wrong with it.

James: You are. Those are boys' clothes, not girls'. You can't wear that, you're a girl. That's for boys. It says so on the label.

Geoff: It doesn't mean you can't wear it.

James: No, but you're making an unnecessary problem with the label.

Geoff: I would say you're making an unnecessary problem doing it the other way.

James: OK. So who does that offend?

Geoff: I don't think anybody has a problem with the boys' section and the girls' section. There's a very small section of society that doesn't think you should genderise anything at all. We have unisex toilets in schools now.

James: Yes, with doors and locks.

Geoff: Well, yeah, again it's not the biggest deal in the world ...

James: OK. This is a little unfair because I appreciate that, historically, you ring in to a radio show and use the phrase 'political correctness' and nobody ever expects you to explain what you mean by it. You just get to bark it or bleat it and get a pat on the back and move along. But why did you ring in? In the great scheme of things that you, Geoff in Macclesfield, care about enough to call in, why this? I appreciate that part of the answer is that you work in the sector, but we've already established that it wouldn't damage your business in any way, shape or form. So pay me the compliment, if you would, of taking a moment now to say to yourself, 'Hang on a minute, why do I care about this so much?'

Geoff: I think you hit the nail on the head. It's about it one day becoming mandatory, becoming illegal to refer to boys and girls separately. I think there's a danger as these things gather momentum of the government stepping in and making laws.

James: I think that's nuts but I respect that you apparently believe it. This is the thin end of a wedge and if we're not careful we'll wake up next week and you won't be able to call yourself a boy or a girl anymore, you'll have to call yourself a person. Just out of interest – and like I said, I think the suggestion's nuts – but if it did happen, how would that affect your sense of self?

Geoff: It wouldn't change my sense of self. I know what I am.

James: So what exactly are you cross about?

Geoff: I wouldn't say I'm cross, I'd say I'm concerned.

James: What are you concerned about then?

Geoff: That these things keep going too far. That people jump on the bandwagon.

James: The only bandwagon I can see here is the one full of people who employ phrases like 'political correctness'. It's kind of the biggest bandwagon of them all. So, just to indulge your slightly odd prediction, imagine I'm in charge and I decide to outlaw the words 'men', 'women', 'girls' and 'boys' and insist instead on the words 'people' and 'children'. You become 'Geoff the person in Macclesfield'. How does that change your sense of self? How does that impact on your life? How does it make your life worse? What is it that you're frightened of?

Geoff: I'm not sure that I've ever really thought about it, because I don't know if I'd allow it to happen.

It's hardly Plato's *Symposium*, I grant you, but Geoff hasn't lazily swallowed this nonsense. He has been so relentlessly and unquestioningly exposed to it for so long that he has never stopped to wonder what he actually, personally means by words he routinely uses. He was a bright, personable and successful businessman who had simply never been asked to have a proper think about where he'd ended up and how he'd ended up there. We parted as friends. I wished him a Happy Winterval.

Chapter 5
FEMINISM

I STILL STRUGGLE TO believe what I'm about to write but recent events have provided pretty incontrovertible evidence that it's true: many apparently straight, unmistakably white men believe that *they* are the real victims of discrimination in the twenty-first-century West. Gays, ethnic minorities, Muslims, transgender activists and, most of all, women are apparently favoured by modern society's structures to an unbearable degree. The 'traditional' male, who wants nothing more than sex on demand, the right to determine his partner's access to contraception and abortion and his dinner on the table when he gets home from work is, in the modern world of equality, feminism and Black Lives Matter, a man indubitably more sinned against than sinning.

As a straight, white man I find this completely absurd, but I no longer find it funny. On 23 April 2018, a 25-year-old computer studies graduate called Alek Minassian drove through Toronto trying to kill people with his van. The terror attack left 10 dead and 16 more seriously injured. Shortly after his arrest,

Minassian introduced many of us to the word 'incel'. Short for 'involuntary celibates', it describes a self-styled group of male supremacists who believe in what the psychology professor and author Jordan Peterson – who, whether by accident or design, is something of a hero to both the so-called 'men's rights' and 'alt-right' movements – has called 'enforced monogamy'. Peterson, who famously believes that the natural state of human hierarchies and relationships would mirror those of lobsters, contends that Minassian 'was angry at God because women were rejecting him. The cure for that is enforced monogamy. That's actually why monogamy emerges.'[*]

A form of 'sexual redistribution', this 'enforced monogamy' is necessary because, according to Peterson, in a world where women are completely free to choose their own sexual partners they will be disproportionately drawn to 'high status' men, meaning that, 'Half the men fail, and no one cares about the men who fail.' I'm not a particular scholar of Peterson's work, but his impact should not be underestimated. His most recent book sold in excess of one million copies and he reportedly earns $80,000 a month from his YouTube channel alone. In other words, he is a Pied Piper of particular and considerable popularity and it behoves us to ask why.

My own theory is that, like Donald Trump, he offers men an excuse for their own failures and absolves them of responsibility

---

[*] 'Jordan Peterson, Custodian of the Patriarchy,' *New York Times*, 18/5/2018.

for their own behaviour. I am, admittedly, not a lobster but I cannot quite believe that you need possess rare skills or charms in order to get a girlfriend. Were I to address the 'involuntary' bit of 'involuntary celibacy', I'd suggest that spending a little less time obsessing online about 'cucks', Muslim 'no-go zones' and 'social justice warriors' would free these most delicate of flowers up to work a little harder at being likeable and hence fanciable.

One of the many contradictions at the heart of this movement is the insistence that men like me, who seek to respect women and try with varying degrees of success to treat them as genuine equals, are somehow 'beta males' while men like them, despite the aridity of their romantic lives, are somehow 'alpha' because they are, I guess, so adept at meting out anonymous online verbal violence. I'd suggest that only men who have had very little to do with the opposite sex could conclude that women are inexorably drawn to 'high status males' but that, when you think about it, is the mother of all chicken-and-egg scenarios.

To our twenty-first-century Western sensibilities, it beggars belief that anybody could seriously argue that women should, regardless of their own feelings, be required to alleviate the sexual frustration of men. But, if we've learned anything over the last few years, it's that progress we once naively believed to be permanent can be easily undone. In many countries, and even in some homegrown religious communities, the perception of a woman as the property of her father and then her husband is still completely entrenched. Despite being relatively well-educated and familiar with the dastardly plots of fictional nineteenth-century villains with evil designs on wards and widows, most of my callers and I still reel at how recently some of the most basic building blocks of sexual equality were put in place. Until the Sex Discrimination Act 1975, fathers and husbands in the UK were routinely required to act as guarantors for women seeking mortgages or credit agreements. Three years after this Act, *The Times* reported that many retailers had retained the practice. For me, examples like this are no longer historical curiosities. Rather, it is evidence that the world people who euphemistically advocate 'traditional gender roles' dream of is not just in the much more recent past than we realise but is also, potentially, in our future. It was not until 1973, for example, that Ireland lifted a ban on married women having jobs (except teaching). Even more pertinent to my point here is the fact that the law was *introduced* in 1933. So much of what I have always taken for granted in the realms of social justice and equality turns out, on cursory examination, to be hard won and, a much tougher lesson, potentially temporary.

If we think of 'enforced monogamy' – or, indeed, voting for a presidential candidate who boasts of 'grabbing' women 'by the pussy' – as being at the peak of Mount Misogyny, then the best way to begin understanding the view of women that spawns such positions is to take a look at how people end up on its nursery slopes. This is entry level male chauvinism, if you like, or the 'everyday sexism' that has provided one of social media's most enlightening threads in recent years. I appreciate that this will probably have scholars of feminism rolling their eyes at the obviousness of it all. But I think a bloke who realised quite late in life that he'd spent years on those slopes, while simultaneously patting himself on the back for being a right-on feminist, provides a useful case study. Obviously, that bloke is me and what follows are the lessons I've learned. It's very much a work in progress.

At its heart, this is an issue of dominion: the belief that men should have complete dominion over women and that a woman's primary purpose is to serve and comfort men. Most men, like me, find it really hard to understand just how systemic this is. We might feel culturally superior to a Saudi Arabian who supports the driving ban on women or morally superior to an 'incel' who thinks it's somehow the sisterhood's fault that he can't get laid, but we're all guilty of similar, albeit smaller, transgressions. The primary driver is sex and the first, really difficult, lesson I learned was how behaviour I once considered utterly normal could be experienced as sexually aggressive.

Fiona was a City lawyer who, when she phoned me a couple of years ago, had been in the job for about 20 years. It was an incident at the very beginning of her career, though, that prompted her to call. We were discussing one of my favourite subjects in this arena, the line between harassment and compliment. It's a conversation that can be inspired by anything from workmen being told off for wolf-whistling to court cases involving behaviour that was once utterly commonplace but is now criminal. I used to think it was very clever to point out to women that they drew this line according to whether or not they were attracted to the man doing the 'compliment-ing', the whistling or even the 'inappropriate touching'. I see now that this involves me putting the responsibility for my behaviour onto them, a process that ultimately led to another female caller, who we'll meet shortly, ringing in to tell me that it is somehow a waitress's fault when she gets groped by a diner.

Fiona: I was doing my articles in a City law firm and one weekend it was just me and a senior partner in the office. It being a Saturday, I was wearing jeans, and when were in the lift together, with no one else, he told me that he loved the way I filled them out.

James: Was he a creep?

Fiona: No. He was incredibly awkward, not just with women, and quite shy. Senior partners in City law firms have a status that leads some of them to be incredibly arrogant and overbearing, but this guy was nothing like them. I've dealt with them too, of course, but it was that thing you said about not knowing when you've crossed the line that made me think of this incident.

James: Lots of people listening will be wondering why you have rung in. I might even be one of them. They'll be thinking that this sounds quite innocuous, especially given that previous callers have described some pretty gross conduct.

Fiona: I know. I didn't know myself at the time why it upset me so much. I certainly didn't feel threatened. But I think I do now. He was telling me, whether he realised it or not, that he had imagined me naked, or at least in just my knickers, and he wanted to tell me how much he'd enjoyed the mental images.

James: Blimey. I've never thought of it like that before. So it disturbed you so much precisely because he defied the stereotype of the workplace loudmouth or the office lothario?

Fiona: Yes. I can't remember how much time we spent in the lift after he said it and I mumbled 'thank you' before giggling like an idiot, but I think I felt shame and I only just worked out why.

James: You realise that he would have had absolutely no idea how you felt? We all know men who revel in making women uncomfortable, who sexualise the most banal exchanges. But from what you've said, he would probably have been absolutely mortified if he'd known how he'd made you feel. I'm not making excuses but he thought he was paying you a compliment.

Fiona: I know. That's why I rang. It's more about the words than the man, sometimes, isn't it?

I still reel from this call, because it exemplifies how something that seems quite banal at first glance can actually end up seeming significant. They're among my favourite moments on the radio because I really feel that I, and so hopefully lots of people listening, am learning something. This was an uncomfortable lesson because I've most certainly said something similar to a woman in the past, probably many times, but it's an important one. The companion piece to Fiona's call is this one with Sheila, who put forward a position I've heard a hundred times, from women older than me.

Sheila: It's ridiculous, James. Men won't be able to pay women a compliment at all soon.

James: Why not?

Sheila: They'll be frightened of getting arrested or sacked, just for saying that they liked a lady's jeans.

James: But he didn't say that he liked her jeans. He said that he liked thinking about the bottom that filled out the jeans. It's the difference between saying 'What a lovely pair of trousers' and 'What a lovely arse'. One seems fine to me, the other really doesn't.

Sheila: Well, I wish men still complimented my arse!

James: Do you, though? Any men? Even the office octopus or the manager with halitosis who breathes down your neck while telling you how sexy you smell? Would you really welcome that?

Sheila: I don't know, but I certainly wouldn't mind getting wolf-whistled once in a while!

Things get quite tricky for me here. I am writing about feminism, claiming to have been on a journey of partial enlightenment, and am now seem poised to explain why I have a better understanding than Sheila of how she should feel about how she is treated by men. Mansplaining, much?

Some women still believe that the policing of bottom-pinching or lewd language or worse is somehow their job. If they are of a robust disposition and think nothing of threatening to punch a bloke who's placed a hand on their knee, they can completely overlook how someone like Fiona felt like in that lift. Worse, some women would even blame her for her own discomfort. She should be 'tougher' seems to be the argument and 'get over herself'. This must be music to a sex pest's ears. But if a woman *doesn't* feel comfortable slapping or chastising or publicly shaming a man who has groped her or propositioned her, then whose job is it? It's increasingly obvious to me that it has to be society's job to establish conventions so clear and so objective that any man behaving like this, whether a Hollywood mogul, a City lawyer or a scaffolder, will be known to have transgressed. We just need to change what is considered to be normal.

Think about what 'normal' behaviour is. Once, it was normal to see doctors advertising cigarettes, to own slaves, to be free to rape your wife. Actually, you couldn't technically rape your wife in the UK until as recently as 1984, when the Criminal Review Committee rejected the idea that 'marital rape' could be a crime. 1984. I was 12. The language is like something from *The Handmaid's Tale*:

> *The majority of us ... believe that rape cannot be considered in the abstract as merely 'sexual intercourse without consent'. The circumstances of rape may be peculiarly grave. This feature is not present in the case of a husband and wife cohabiting with each other when an act of sexual intercourse occurs without the wife's consent. They may well have had sexual intercourse regularly before the act in question and, because a sexual relationship may involve a degree of compromise, she may sometimes have agreed only with some reluctance to such intercourse. Should he go further and force her to have sexual intercourse without her consent, this may evidence a failure of the marital relationship. But it is far from being the 'unique' and 'grave' offence described earlier. Where the husband goes so far as to cause injury, there are available a number of offences against the person with which he may be charged, but the gravamen of the husband's conduct is the injury he has caused, not the sexual intercourse he has forced.*[*]

It's learning things like this – and again it's on Wikipedia, you don't have to be Rumpole of the Bailey to know it – that

---

[*] The Criminal Law Revision Committee Report on Sexual Offences, 1984.

really focuses my mind on the notion that some of the people we work and live alongside would welcome a return to those days. What's described above is, after all, 'enforced monogamy' by any other name. It's an incel's dream and it was legal reality when I was 12 years old.

Most accounts of how societies fall to fascism cite rampant sexism as a key indicator. Not that long ago I found use of the f-word in this context a little fanciful. It seemed to me that modern British and American people were somehow made of different stuff to the Germans who enabled and executed Nazism in the 1930s. But then Donald Trump started separating children from their parents and locking them in cages in latter day concentration camps. Support for the practice, heartbreakingly widespread on both sides of the Atlantic, seemed to come largely from people who also subscribed to fascistic attitudes regarding immigrants in general, Muslims in particular, homosexuals and transsexuals. It no longer looks fanciful to put independent, sexually autonomous women on the list. These are same the people, after all, who cite 'forced marriage' and the hideously misnomered 'honour killings' as evidence that Muslims are fundamentally different from the rest of us. It is always fruitful to point out to them that a forced marriage is pivotal to the plot of Romeo and Juliet and that Henry the Eighth is probably history's most famous proponent of honour killings.

And you can only understand how women can end up on such a list if you dig down in to another one of those words we all routinely use and hear without ever really pausing to consider its proper meaning: objectification. Literally the action of degrading someone to the status of a mere object, when applied to women it provides the key to understanding why I, as a man, have not only a right but even a duty to insist that women should not be 'free to choose' to do certain things. I am incredibly conscious of how thin the ice beneath my feet becomes when I write something like that, but my biggest breakthrough came in 2018 when two rather different stories seemed to me to speak to exactly the same issue.

In January, the *Financial Times* journalist Madison Marriage went to work undercover as a 'hostess' at something called the Presidents Club Dinner. Described, inevitably, as 'the most un-PC event of the year' and held at London's ineffably grand Dorchester Hotel, it saw 360 of the country's wealthiest men, a couple of politicians and a few celebrities being 'entertained' by 130 'hostesses' in uniforms of short dresses and high heels. The undercover investigation revealed that hostesses were routinely groped and harassed at a drunken after-party, while one auction prize offered plastic surgery to 'spice up your wife'.

And so it continued. The women, who had been required by the event organisers to sign a five-page non-disclosure agreement at the beginning of the evening, queued up to tell the *Financial Times* about being groped, grabbed, pawed, propositioned and treated, in other words, like nothing more than sex objects. That the culprits supposedly represented the 'great and the good' perhaps explains why some of my callers initially tried to defend the sleazebags' conduct and I had a bit of fun listening to their spluttering confusion when asked whether they would have felt the same way had the offenders been, say, minicab drivers of Pakistani origin. It was a woman, though, who for me best highlighted the importance of leaving the drawing of lines to society itself as opposed to the individual women involved. There is rather more of me than her in this exchange, embarrassingly, but that's because I was literally trying to work out what to think as we spoke. Lorraine had some experience of the sector, and had arranged events herself, so was sceptical of the idea that the behaviour at the dinner was especially egregious. Again, the difficulty of persuading someone that something which has always been *normal* to them is actually utterly outrageous comes to the fore. We began by examining the *FT*'s report that one society figure told a hostess: 'You look far too sober ... I want you to down that glass, rip off your knickers and dance on that table.'

Lorraine: What? Somebody said that to a girl and she didn't complain on the night? Well more fool her.

James: But now you're making her responsible, Lorraine.

Lorraine: Well she has to take some responsibility.

James: She's frightened, she's at the Dorchester, she's surrounded by rich and powerful men. She's signed a five-page document promising not to tell tales and not to complain.

This is where I think, despite me being a bloke and you being a woman, we're looking through different ends of the same telescope. I could never hear a tale of a woman being badly treated by a man and think, 'Oh I'm going to say something negative about the woman.'

Lorraine: Look. I think what's happened here is, had this molestation happened in a park, then quite right do what you need to do, but it happened on a charity evening, when the girls know the men are going to be sat there having drinks, laughing and joking ...

James: Woah. Again, I'm sorry but this is what we have to change. That blithe acceptance that you just articulated. 'Oh, it's going to happen so we should just accept it.' No! No! No!

Lorraine: Well, then, what will happen in the future is men will be so frightened to go to charity evenings that charities will suffer and not get the funds they deserve.

James: What will they be frightened of?

Lorraine: They'll be frightened of being accused of something that never happened or something that did happen and should have been dealt with on the spot.

James: How do you extrapolate from a story about women being molested and abused that men who have never molested or abused women have somehow got something to fear? How do you even do that, Lorraine?

Lorraine: Because where does the line get drawn?

James: The line gets drawn, Lorraine, between men who have done it and men who have not.

Lorraine: And the men who have not, right, will be nervous about going to charity events in the future?

James: Well, I am a man who has not and I can tell you categorically that you're wrong. If men who molest women at an event are hauled over the coals, I am not going to be worried that I might go to a party and be wrongly accused of sticking my hand up a waitress's skirt. Because I know that I am never going to stick my hand up a waitress's skirt. And what you do when you make it about the men – and I know you don't intend this – but you tell men that this sort of behaviour is somehow OK and that it's the woman's job to decide what isn't.

Lorraine: Well, I certainly wouldn't do that.

James: You just did! Come on. If we start coming down like a ton of bricks on men who stick their hands up a girl's skirt then men who have never stuck their hands up a girl's skirt are going to be worried that they might be accused of sticking their hands up a girl's skirt?

(You'll notice that I've started describing these young women as girls. Nobody's perfect. I told you this was a work in progress.)

Lorraine: You've just confirmed my point, James.

James: No, I've just repeated your point back to you in the hope that you'd realise how vile it was. But you clearly don't.

Lorraine: Well, believe me, having run a charity for so long and doing so much hard work, without the girls' help it would not have happened. And if any of my girls had been in that situation on any evening that we did, I *would* have come down on the men responsible like a ton of bricks.

James: Well hang on, you cannot come down on them like a ton of bricks, because then next year all the men who have never molested a woman in their life would be worried, under your logic, that they were going to be accused of sticking their hand up a waitress's skirt.

Lorraine: No, because I would not have made it so public.

James: So just a little word in their ear, then? That's right?

Lorraine: No, no, no. He would have been taken to one side and spoken to by security and asked to leave. And then he would have been banned from any future events.

James: But that would mean that next year all the other men would be worried that they were going to be accused even when they hadn't done anything wrong.

Lorraine: We wouldn't have made it public like this.

James: I see. So you behave honourably, but you do it in secret?

> **Lorraine:** I think, you know, there's always two sides to every story and to make it so public, James, I just think it's wrong.
>
> **James:** Well it was the *Financial Times* that made it public.

I'm not completely naive. I know stuff like this goes on up and down the country. I have been to lap-dancing clubs. I even attended, as callow cub reporter, what the sports desk at the *Daily Express* referred to as a 'gentlemen's evening', which Caligula would have found a little strong for his tastes. But as I get older and recognise that I've spent most of my life utterly oblivious to the offences and abuses that women endure on a daily basis, I realise that men won't change until society changes and, right now, forces seem to be trying to pull society backwards as well as forwards. In the aftermath of this scandal, for example, I learned that Section 40 of the Equality Act 2010, which required employers to safeguard employees against harassment from clients and customers, had been repealed in 2013 as part of the Conservative Party's tabloid-friendly programme of 'cutting red tape'.

Perhaps the biggest catalyst for social change in recent years is the #MeToo movement which saw scores of Hollywood actresses come forward to describe the sexual abuse they had allegedly suffered at the hands of an incredibly powerful producer. It seemed to signal a sea change in sexual politics that will hopefully resonate for generations to come and prompted women a million miles away from Hollywood to speak out about the climate of casual abuse in which they had always lived. I was staggered to learn from callers, and from women I know and love in my personal life, how 'normal' it was for a boss to squeeze their breast during a drunken staff photo or how often they've had to fight off colleagues at a Christmas party. The inchoate anger some men feel at not only having to check their objectification but also to accept that only a woman gets to decide when a woman has sex, is one of the ugliest phenomena at loose in the world today. The misogyny and abuse directed at women online is toxic in the extreme, and female MPs routinely receive rape threats. Determination to combat it should be fuelled by the knowledge that it is not new and, until very recently, these men really did have everything their own way. As with every other philosophy built upon the idea that straight, white men are somehow victims of twenty-first-century mores, they dream of an indistinct but not-too-distant past. I suspect this is why anger levels can go stratospheric when that past seems to be slipping a little further away.

About a fortnight after the Presidents Club scandal, and with many of its attendant issues still exercising commentators and columnists, the company running Formula 1 motor racing announced that they were doing away with 'grid girls' – traditionally attractive young women in skimpy and/or national costume who would hang around the race track carrying umbrellas and being ornamental. The new owner of Formula 1, Liberty Media Corporation, almost certainly made the decision in the hope of attracting a younger, more female audience to the sport. It was, therefore, a reflection of an already changing society. In the eyes of the professionally furious and aggrieved, however, it was yet more evidence of everything from political correctness going mad (again) to the continuing triumphant march of the radical killjoy feminist.

I'd like to point out here that I'd spent my life never questioning the appropriateness or otherwise of scantily-clad women waving cards around in a boxing ring or accompanying darts players to the oche. But with my newly forged belief that you won't reduce harassment and abuse until you wipe out institutional objectification, I approached the saga of the so-called 'grid girls' with a new found determination to ensure that guardians of 'traditional' objectification understood and had to explain precisely what it was they were defending.

Peter rang from Monte Carlo to patronise me ever so charmingly and condemn the decision, while explaining that although they were much more than mere ornamentation he would not personally miss them. I responded by asking him *why* he thought they were there on the grid in the first place.

> **Peter:** I don't think. I *know*. They were there because, before the statement made this week by Liberty, they were seen to be an intrinsic part of the show.

James: But why are they an intrinsic part of the show? I'm not trying to trip you up or anything. I want to know why they're there. If I had to explain it to a young woman in particular – or a young boy – why are they there, Peter?

Peter: I can only answer that by saying that, like many other sports and many other activities, it has become a tradition and a part of the show.

James: So why do you want them to stay there, even though you've said that they won't affect your enjoyment of the show in an way, shape or form. And I don't think that's true. You do like looking at them don't you?

Peter: Why do you want them to go?

James: I don't have a strong view one way or another. I'm trying to understand why they're there.

Peter: [sighs] I'll repeat what I said the last time. It's tradition.

James: I know what you said the last time, but there's loads of traditions. It used to be a tradition to send kids up chimneys, but you wouldn't defend that on the grounds that we've always done it, otherwise you'd end up being an apologist for everything from slavery to women not having the vote. I know it went on in the past. And it looks like it won't happen in the future. So let's focus on the last race you went to. Why were they there?

Peter: As I said to you and I'll repeat again—

James: Come on, Peter. What is the rationale for them being there? You can't have a rationale that just says they always were. So why were they there, Peter?

Peter: They weren't grid girls, originally, they were promotional girls for large corporations, mainly those selling cigarettes, and that is when you did see them rushing around in bikinis.

James: So that's not why they're there now then?

Peter: It grew out of America, where there were grid girls.

James: Why were they there?

Peter: You'll have to ask them.

James: But I'm asking you, because you're defending it without knowing why it exists.

Peter: You're making it very difficult for me, because I'm trying to explain to you what it's grown out of and you're saying 'forget the past'. Well, unfortunately many things are based on the past, and there are progressions.

James: I completely agree with you, and that is what progress means. It's recognising that things from the past should probably be changed. I will ask you once more, and I'm sorry that you feel this is an unfair question, but I'm only asking it again and again because I'm fascinated to hear the answer. Why are they there?

Peter: [sighs] Why is the earth round?

James: OK, Peter.

Peter: You cannot ask me to tell you what was in the mind of the management who organised it.

James: I know. I just want to hear your own reason in your own head. Because I think I know why they're there. I think they're there to, sort of, titillate sad old men.

Peter: Well, then maybe you're a sad old man.

James: Maybe, but at least I've got an answer to the question. Why do you think they're there?

Peter: Well I don't think they're there to titillate sad old men.

James: So that's a no. We can cross that off the list. What are we going to put on the list instead?

Peter: So why shouldn't you add a bit of glamour to a sporting event?

James: So it is to titillate sad old men?

Peter: No. Because sad old men are not … are not …

James: So they're there to add glamour to a sporting event?

Peter: Yes.

James: That's fine. I've got it. It's not difficult, but it's like pulling teeth with you, Peter! But just to clarify, your enjoyment of the sporting event is not going to be in any way diminished when they're not there. You did say that, right?

Peter: No. You asked about enjoyment. I will still continue to watch the event.

James: But you'll enjoy it a bit less?

> **Peter:** Not necessarily.
>
> **James:** So you won't enjoy it less?
>
> **Peter:** No.

I am all too aware that I sometimes come across as an insufferable prig in exchanges like this, though I prefer the 'dog with a bone' simile. I think it's important to press on because, as Peter unintentionally explained, progressions from the past are possible and I don't know how they can ever be achieved without first acknowledging that they are necessary. I was a bit more sledgehammer than scalpel in this conversation, but that's the only weapon I've currently got against intransigence – an abject refusal to answer a question honestly because the interlocutor is bright enough to realise that to do so would paint him in a bad light. I hope to develop new ones.

To answer the question Peter preferred not to answer, grid girls attended Formula 1 races because previous generations believed it perfectly acceptable to value, pay and display women according *entirely* to their physical appearance. It reduced them to ornamental objects. It's commonplace to see people argue that objecting to this sort of objectification necessarily entails condemning make-up or bikinis. They even argue that the position denies the basic fact that human beings find each other physically attractive and so try to enhance our physical charms by whatever means. This is surely nonsense. Grid girls and darts walk-on girls and Presidents Club hostesses reflect a society that believes it is normal to value a woman according *only* to how she looks. I don't want to live in such a society. I want to live in a society that recognises physical appearance to be an intrinsic part of who we are, without supporting the notion that it is the only thing that matters. By contrast, a society that reflects a belief that sexuality or physicality has no place at all in the public space ends up with burkhas, niqabs and segregation. It's not about lap-dancing clubs or burlesque shows or pornography either, it's about what happens in that public space. Of all the things I think I'm right about, though, this has been the hardest to arrive at. It remains a work in progress.

Chapter 6
NANNY STATES AND CLASSICAL LIBERALS

FIXED-ODDS BETTING TERMINALS CHANGED everything for me. I've never played one, though. This isn't a tale of penury or bankruptcy brought on by addiction to what has become known as the 'crack cocaine of gambling'. Rather, it is an account of how the gaming machines, which first appeared in British bookmakers in 2002, make a mockery of libertarian arguments against government intervention in the private lives and personal choices of citizens.

Libertarians are an increasingly populous tribe. Twitter, for example, groans under the weight of borderline sociopaths and assorted self-important weirdos who describe themselves as 'libertarian' or, even worse, 'classically liberal'. Their uniting belief seems to be that because they are apparently capable of avoiding the dangerous consequences of unfettered 'free choice' – addiction, obesity, death, etc – governments should not spend money helping less educated, less disciplined and almost always less wealthy people do the same. It sits very comfortably with the weapons-grade free market position that nothing should ever be done in law to curtail the ability of businesses to make as much profit as possible. In many ways, these positions are two cheeks of the same backside and both use the pejorative 'nanny state' to malign the idea that lawmakers should ever endeavour to protect people from themselves and the multifarious pitfalls of modern life.

Like 'virtue signalling', a term which seeks to ridicule the ideas of altruism and generosity by suggesting that they are only ever undertaken in search of admiration, the phrase 'nanny state' seems to have first appeared in the pages of the right-wing *Spectator* magazine. Both terms seek to camouflage crass selfishness by dressing it up in pseudo-intellectual language, invariably informed by a resentment of tax revenues being spent on things of no immediate benefit to these particular taxpayers. And both conspire to create an environment in which you can be easily portrayed as a sandal-wearing, muesli-munching do-gooder if you think legal limits should be placed on either corporate greed or a person's ability to do harm to themselves and their families. In the long term, of course, the happier, healthier and wealthier a population is, the less strain it will place on the public purse. But the long-term welfare of the entire population is traditionally of little interest to the parts of it keenest to see taxes cut and shareholder dividends soar.

Anyway, back to the bookies. The first thing you learn when you start speaking to people who have fallen under the spell of fixed-odds betting terminals, or FOBTs, is that they are nothing like traditional fruit machines. We are all familiar with the siren lure in the corner of the pub, where flashing lights and cartoon characters promise jackpots and fun. The FOBT is an altogether different beast. Middle-class British high streets increasingly seem to be populated exclusively by coffee shops, estate agents and chain restaurants. In the poorer parts of town, fast food joints and betting shops have assumed a comparable dominance. This has nothing to do with the popularity horse racing or any other sport, as I used to innocently believe. In short, the revenues raised by a brace of fixed-odds betting terminals in each shop is invariably enough to pay staff and rent while leaving a tidy profit for the bookmaker's shareholders.

They work so 'well' because they use some of the starkest teachings of behaviourist psychology. The 'fixed odds' element of the equation sees the punter make regular small wins as he plays, in pretty much the perfect proportion to ensure that he keeps playing. Next, the games' designers ensure that the gap between wins never becomes big enough to sate his hunger for the next payout. And finally, with the psychological trap so perfectly set, you allow him to stake as much as £100 every twenty seconds. This combination of frequent wins, massive stakes and incredibly quick gameplay mean that these machines are designed to maximise the amount of time that people play for. And the more they play, the more they lose. In academic language, this process has become known as state-corporate harm maximisation.

The machines are deliberately located in the poorest parts of towns (there is a reason why they have been referred to as a 'class-targeted form of gambling'). Granted, no one needs to cross the threshold of the bookmakers and, if they do, nobody is forcing you to put any money in one of these machines. Also, plenty of people will have done both without falling foul of any addictive behaviour or seeing their life savings drain away at a rate of knots. And yet, the point, as I have come to see it, is that the choice being exercised here is actually anything but free. Huge amounts of revenue and effort have been expended on creating a machine that is literally designed to *maximise* the harm it does to its users. Next to nothing has been spent on seeking to redress the balance, seeking not even to *minimise* the harm but merely to alleviate some of it.

In May 2018, the UK government acknowledged this when it pledged to make bookmakers reduce the maximum stake from £100 to £2. Shortly afterwards it was reported that, after pressure from the gambling industry, this would be delayed for two years. We shall have to wait and see. But the lesson FOBTs have taught me will remain in place, regardless of whether the legislation ever appears. It completely revolutionised my understanding of the term 'free choice' and, I think, my politics.

I remember making a rare foray into my student union at the London School of Economics. Oddly, for someone who loved debating at school and went on to make a career out of arguing with people, I wasn't interested in student politics. Its most enthusiastic practitioners seemed either old and bitter beyond their years on the right, or angry about everything on the left. *Plus ça change!* On this occasion, the debate had something to do with abolishing unemployment benefit. Embarrassingly, I was on it at the time, having failed my first year exams, and so decided to chip in to the debate. Using myself as an example of someone who would have had to leave university if I'd not been able to access some sort of state support, I explained how I had already secured part-time work and would, on graduating, probably be a much more productive tax payer with a degree than I would have been without.

Being a stranger to the union's traditions, I hopped off the stage and sat down in the middle of what turned out to be the university's small band of hard right, free marketeers. 'If you can't afford to be here,' spat one of them, with real disgust on his face, 'you should get a proper job and leave.' This, remember, was when everything university-related was still pretty much free, and decades before tuition fees became a political hot potato. It's taken me years to realise that this was probably my first introduction to the ideological selfishness peculiar to a certain brand of Conservatism.

I was always taught to be grateful for what I had and to be mindful of those less fortunate. These lessons came mostly from Mum and Dad, but it's possible that being educated in Catholic schools amplified these messages. That certainly contributed to the feelings of guilt that kick in when you do things you know to be wrong. For good or for ill, then, I grew up feeling lucky and blessed. Being adopted probably played a part, too. It happened when I was 28 days old and I've always been aware of it, but I wonder today whether it gives you an inner duality absent in most conventional family structures. As a boy, I thought a lot about the me who didn't get adopted. That boy would have been raised in care or by a teenage single mother, shamed by the stigma of my existence in an Ireland still under the jackboot of the clergy. He would not have had my education or enjoyed the emotional and material security that came from being raised by two comfortably off, deeply loving parents in a happy home. I hope my politics is selfless, but when I think about it this way I wonder whether there's a degree of secondhand selfishness involved.

The philosopher John Rawls' famous 'veil of ignorance' posits the idea that a just system can only be constructed by people completely ignorant of their position within it. In other words, you're not going to endorse a system of law (or, by extension, of tax or government) that unfairly discriminates against a section of society you could conceivably be in yourself. I simplify outrageously, but my 'veil of adoption' makes me imagine that it's me with a different backstory tempted by the get-rich-quick lies of a FOBT, or the temporary hit to my brain's pleasure centre provided by a cigarette. Perhaps it's fanciful, but I find it very easy to imagine the unadopted me falling foul of the myriad financial, medical and chemical bear traps laid by champions of state-corporate harm maximisation. And so, when it comes to the so-called 'nanny state', I cut my political cloth accordingly.

As with every other divisive and dangerous school of thought, from racism to homophobia and back again, adherents to 'classical liberalism' also get to mask their own feelings of inadequacy and self-loathing by casting themselves as somehow inherently superior to other humans. Loosely put, it posits the notion that all people are essentially selfish and calculating and that government is only needed to protect us from each other rather than from ourselves. Further, the influence of government or the state should extend no further than protecting a population from its feral, pre-society natural state. An essential prerequisite of fascism, the idea that a person's 'quality' is somehow defined by their birth, gets employed here to attempt moral justification of epic inequality. If you can't afford to go to university then you are obviously not university material and a university education would be wasted on you. The idea that superior *I* should not somehow see my taxes subsidising inferior *you* is thus easy to sustain. I suspect it's also why so many right-wing inheritors of wealth and status cling so desperately to the notion that they have somehow 'earned' or 'deserved' their privilege, rather than arrived at it through dumb luck. Americans sum it up best when they talk of people who 'were born on third base but go through life thinking they hit a triple'.

Proponents of 'nanny state' rhetoric – call them classical liberals, free marketeers or just plain selfish – generally fall into two categories. First, those 'third basers', the beneficiaries of entrenched and inherited inequality who seek to persuade themselves and others that these inequalities are not only justified but also somehow natural. This attempt to render in-built unfairness as 'natural', incidentally, explains why some of them end up flirting with eugenics. Second, the constituency of people on the wrong side of the inequality who support the structure in the almost always mistaken belief that they might somehow end up among the 'winners'. They're best described in another American adage, often wrongly attributed to John Steinbeck, which describes poor people who 'see themselves not as an exploited proletariat but as temporarily embarrassed millionaires.'

I don't know for sure whether Henry in Fulham belongs in the first or second category, but I'd put money on it being the first. He called in during a conversation about a then-notional 'sugar tax' which the British government would bring into law in April 2018. The idea is that a levy on sugary drinks (there are seven teaspoons of sugar in a 330ml can of cola) will encourage companies to use less sugar and, if they persist, the monies raised through the extra taxation can be used to offset the cost of treating the many health issues arising from excessive sugar consumption. What's not to like? Well, for the Henrys of this world, and for their spiritual leaders in various think tanks and pressure groups who argue in defence of economic 'freedom', the answer is quite a lot. A sugar tax does three things these people hate. It challenges the idea that companies should be free to do whatever they want to get ever more money out of customers and, further, it promotes the notion that the state should actively seek to counterbalance unfettered capitalism. And, of course, it obviously takes a potential bite out of shareholders' profits, but I think in this case the social and political implications stick in their collective craw more than the purely financial ones.

James: What's not to like?

Henry: Why should I pay more because other people are too stupid to understand that they're going to get diabetes if they drink a gallon of pop for breakfast?*

James: Is that really how it works, though? How will the sugar tax you pay end up helping people drink less pop? I thought the idea was that, if the pop costs more, then people will drink less of it?

Henry: No. If I want to buy a can of my favourite pop, which I drink occasionally and in moderation, I would have to pay more for it because some people don't understand that if they drink loads of it they will get fat and ill. I am paying more tax so that they drink less pop.

James: OK. You're right. Can you afford to pay a few pence more every time you buy a can of pop?

Henry: That's not the point.

James: Maybe not, but it's the question I'm asking. Can you?

Henry: Of course I can. So can you.

James: Obviously. In fact, I could probably pay about double what a can currently costs without it having any noticeable impact on, say, my weekly expenditure. Could you?

---

* He didn't actually say 'pop', if memory serves. He didn't ring in from the pages of an Enid Blyton book or my Midlands childhood. I'm cunningly avoiding legal action from the owners of the brand he did mention by leaving it out of this exchange.

Henry: It depends how much I drink.

James: I know. You said 'occasionally and in moderation' a minute ago, though, so we've got a fair idea of the answer. You could do, right?

Henry: Yes.

James: So, any sugar tax on fizzy drinks would have, at the very worst, a negligible effect on your personal finances, but you care enough about it to ring a radio show. Can I ask why?

Henry: Because it's a slippery slope. If we start putting taxes on unhealthy things because some people are too stupid to realise they're unhealthy then where will it end?

James: With taxes on tobacco and alcohol?

Henry: They're not the same but, yes, I'd prefer a government that didn't try to use taxation to give health and safety lessons to voters.

James: Let's go back a bit. You said that you didn't want the money you wouldn't notice paying being used to help people who *didn't understand* the health implications of guzzling loads of sugar. You also called them stupid, but let's focus on the idea that they don't understand. How come you do understand, Henry?

Henry: It's common sense.

James: It's not though, is it? It's something you learned. Either at school or because you are exposed to media and information that covers the issue?

Henry: Not necessarily.

James: It's not a trick question. Either this knowledge, this understanding, this absence of stupidity, arrived in your consciousness by a form of magic or divine intervention, or you somehow *learned* that there is loads of sugar in fizzy drinks and so drinking them is really, really bad for you.

Henry: We did an experiment at school where a penny put in a beaker of cola would dissolve completely in about a week. Everyone did.

James: Well, everyone didn't. People who went to schools like mine and yours will have done, but that's far from everybody. Anyway, I thought that was more about the damage it does to your teeth. I think I'm older than you, but I don't remember diabetes or obesity or heart disease getting a mention. But I digress. How did you find out that too many sugary drinks could cause obesity and diabetes?

Henry: I don't know.

James: But you're adamant that the pittance you might pay in sugar tax, if it ever comes in, is an assault on your freedom because it might somehow help people who've never learned the lesson to be a bit thinner and healthier?

Henry: That's not what I said.

James: It totally is.

In retrospect, Sunny Delight should have sounded a much louder alarm. A concoction so garishly orange that many people believed it might actually cause the sort of skin tone Donald Trump would later popularise, it arrived on our shores in April 1998. By August 1999, a £10 million promotional campaign featuring fresh-faced, wholesome children guzzling the stuff while, probably abseiling and bull-fighting, had installed it as the third most popular soft drink in the country. Only Coke and Pepsi were selling more. It was even, briefly, the twelfth bestselling grocery product in the country. The manufacturers, Proctor & Gamble, insisted that it be sold in supermarket chiller cabinets alongside fruit juice, lulling parents who cared about such things into believing that it was a healthy alternative to fizzy pop. But it wasn't.

When it emerged that Sunny Delight consisted of about 5 per cent fruit and 95 per cent water and high-fructose corn syrup, the drink fell from grace almost as quickly as it had risen. The recently founded Food Commission, a not-for-profit company that campaigns for healthier food, pronounced Sunny Delight to be a 'con', with particular criticism aimed at the way putting it in chiller cabinets had encouraged the erroneous belief that it had any nutritional content worth preserving. Then, in what must rank as one of the biggest marketing disasters of the modern age, it really did turn a girl 'orangey-yellow'. Admittedly, the four-year-old from Rhyl in Wales was necking 1.5 litres of the stuff every day, but the damage was done and sales had halved by 2001.

This story, I realise now, was way ahead of its time. It gives the lie to Henry's notion that you have to be stupid not to appreciate the potential harm a product can do, because it highlights so perfectly how much effort and expenditure is invested in making us believe that said product is not just not harmful, but actively beneficial. The choice of whether to buy something or not cannot be really 'free' if on one side a multinational conglomerate is spending millions upon millions of pounds persuading parents to pour it down their children's throats, while on the other, if we're lucky, a tiny not-for-profit campaign group is trying to be heard. And, of course, it's not just the money spent on conventional advertising. The commercial clout these companies exert stretches into almost every corner of modern life, from product placement in popular TV shows to the sponsorship of major sporting events.

The chef and campaigner Jamie Oliver, who I'm proud to consider a friend, endures untold abuse from the usual corners of the media for his insistence that people need help to make the 'right' choices. It is, apparently, 'sneering' and 'condescending' to use your passion, public profile, knowledge and expertise to help people who have less of the above live longer, happier lives. More than anyone else in the UK, he has succeeded in forcing the issue of 'free' choice being anything but into the light and persuading politicians to contemplate action. The sugar tax was a personal victory for him, but it constitutes a tiny part of what he sees as necessary to safeguard the nation's health.

Back in 2014, for example, Oliver first mooted the idea that fast food joints should not be allowed to open within 'spitting distance' of schools. Cambridge University research shows that people living closest to the largest number of takeaway food outlets were more than twice as likely to be obese. As takeaway outlets proliferate and our children get visibly and statistically bigger, so a similar link with schools seems hard to resist. But not to Gary in Staines.

Gary: It's none of Jamie Oliver's business what my kids eat.

James: Whose business is it then?

Gary: Mine. And their mum's. And theirs.

James: OK. Do they take packed lunches into school?

Gary: They've left school now but no, they didn't. They both had school dinners.

James: And who decided what was on the school dinner menu? You, your wife or your kids?

Gary: If I told you my wife was a dinner lady, would you believe me?

James: No, mate.

Gary: Fair enough. The dinner ladies decided what they had for dinner, I suppose.

James: Right. So it is actually someone else's business what your kids eat. And it's not the dinner ladies that decide. More often than not, as you'd know if you'd seen Jamie Oliver's series about it, they just heat up and serve stuff that's centrally sourced and selected chiefly for being as cheap as chips. That's how they ended up eating Turkey Twizzlers and all the other rubbish. And guess what?

Gary: What?

James: The people deciding what to feed your kids don't actually care one jot about their health. They make their decisions based on what will see the most money left over from the school catering contract for the company's shareholders. If you want your children to get healthy school meals, you literally have to prise the whole process away from the people who see an opportunity to make a quick buck from the feeding them crud.

Gary: What's that got to do with fast food joints?

James: Well, they don't care about your kids' health either, but how many adverts and billboards do you think kids come across every day that make burgers and fried chicken and pizza and fizzy drinks look tempting?

Gary: No idea.

James: Think about it. Billboards, adverts in the bus stops, adverts on telly, adverts in the cinema, adverts when they're watching sport on telly, billboards in the background when they're watching sport on telly, posters at train stations, adverts on trains. You've seen these things?

Gary: Yes. Of course.

James: And now make a list of all the things on the other side of the fence – all the billboards they might regularly come across that try to teach them that the burgers, chicken, pizza and pop are bad for them. All the ads telling them to neck *less* of the stuff instead of as much as possible. What have you got?

Gary: Yeah, right.

James: Seriously. What have you got?

Gary: Not a lot.

James: You haven't, mate. It's not a fair fight. But there is at least someone pretty powerful on the other side, trying to get your kids to eat less of the stuff that could make them fat and poorly. You know who I'm talking about, don't you?

Gary: Jamie Oliver.

It goes further than just the quantity of messaging as well, the quality seems crucial too. Imagine a put-upon mum who is vaguely aware of public health pronouncements concerning junk food and sugar. She's short of cash and hates nothing more than buying her child something that the child won't eat. What messages is she receiving as she wheels the pushchair home from the bus stop?

The bus stop itself, obviously, is adorned with a picture of golden fried chicken breasts, drumsticks, chips and a cob of comedy sweetcorn. The fizzy drink served alongside would, when I was a child in 1970s, have been more than enough for our family of four – today it is a single serving. The child, perhaps, has picked up advertising slogans from the TV and sings the one associated with the chicken chain or the burger chain on the 30-foot hoarding they walk past on the way under the railway bridge. Call it a 15-minute walk in an urban area and just count all the ads and billboards. But they're only the tip of the iceberg.

As mentioned in regard to the FOBTs, high streets in areas of lower wealth are increasingly dominated by takeaway outlets, so much so that I sometimes wonder how they all make a profit. How many will our notional mother pass before she gets home? And how hard would it be for her to believe that anything so widespread, so easily accessible and so popular could be seriously harmful? I don't think this is patronising or 'middle class'. It's a simple acknowledgment of how common it is to live in an environment where the cheapest, most heavily promoted and most unhealthy food and drinks available are by far the most readily available.

The smaller, independent outlets where post-school 'specials' are the norm and children can fill themselves with carbohydrates, fat and unidentified fried protein for a couple of quid are not the source of the problem. They are, to badly paraphrase Eric Cantona, the seagulls that follow the trawler of free market 'classical liberal' big business. Having spoken to countless Garys and mums like the one in our example,

I now see no difference between the psychological engineering of an FOBT and the industrial-scale marketing of food and drink that is shortening life expectancy for the first time in history.

Right-wing newspapers, as ever, make everything worse. In March 2018, the employers' group Business in the Community, in conjunction with Public Health England, published a pack of ideas designed to help employers improve the health of their workforce. It could have been deliberately designed to twitch the outrage antennae of the 'nanny state' critics. One of the suggestions was to 'Begin a conversation about how special events (birthdays, holidays, anniversaries, promotions) are marked at work. Can "cake days" be shared, or healthier alternatives provided?' Even more shockingly, the guide proposed offering free fruit and vegetables around the workplace instead of employees bringing in sugary 'treats'.

By the time it had been run through the mangle of the modern media, this worthy but well-meaning idea had been turned into a 'ban on birthday cakes'. The *Daily Express* even sent a reporter to deliver a cake to 'the killjoy health bosses who are trying to ban birthday treats in the workplace'. There is a tragic piquancy to the tweet that Public Health England (PHE) felt compelled to issue after the newspapers had filled their proverbial boots. 'Today's newspapers are wrong,' it said, 'We are not banning cake.' Columnists and commentators had particular fun noting that PHE, an executive agency of the Department of Health and Social Care, employed 5,000 people to come up with this sort of 'tosh'. A few days later it emerged that, far from being in the business of just banning cakes, PHE also had responsibility for issues such as advising the general public on how to deal with a suspected nerve agent attack in Salisbury. At this point, the columnists and commentators looked the other way.

So there are a few strands here, but I think it's possible to tie them all together. Fans of unfettered free markets balk at the notion of governments interfering in the breakneck pursuit of profit at any (legal) cost. 'Classical liberals' are similarly perturbed by the idea that they should have to moderate their behaviour or pay taxes in order to help a section of the population to which they don't belong. The two combine to create a society in which money is all that matters, but in which 'freedom of choice' is used as a fig leaf to camouflage a callous commitment to an economic system which further enriches the already rich at the expense of the eternally poor.

If a government spends money encouraging our notional mum to give her child tap water instead of a sweetened successor to Sunny Delight, nobody makes a buck. If a government seeks to limit the amount of advertising promoting such products, the ability to make a buck might be compromised, so the newspapers owned by plutocrats with fingers in countless commercial pies line up to decry the 'nanny state'. If fast food joints are prevented from opening up within a 400 metre radius of a school, then it is an unconscionable assault on business and free choice. In other words, companies should be free to employ every tactic under the sun to get us to do ourselves harm if there's money it for them; but if a politician, a celebrity chef or a journalist suggests that tax revenues should be spent or decisions taken to alleviate some of that harm, then it is KILLJOY DO-GOODERS USHERING IN THE NANNY STATE BECAUSE POLITICAL CORRECTNESS HAS GONE MAD! (Again.)

Oddly, it was at Bangkok Airport that everything fell into place. I had an ear infection, mild jet lag and a couple of hours to kill so I wandered the terminal in an almost trance-like state of contemplation. I ended up at a stand for ice cream that is a household name in America and is sold in various-sized tubs. The pricing hypnotised me. Like a stoned student trying to choose a packet of crisps, I stared at the display for what felt like ages, because the massive tub was only a bit more expensive than the smallest and I couldn't work out why. Consider now that the ice cream in question would consist mostly of sugar and fat. The costs of getting it from factory to customer would see transport, staff, promotion and premises rent far outweigh the cost of actually making the stuff. In fact, I realised, it cost so little to produce that once the other costs had been factored into the price of the smallest portion, any money spent on more ice cream would be almost pure profit. The pricing was literally designed to make me think that I was getting a bargain if I bought a gallon, and ripped off if I bought the smallest (least unhealthy) portion. I bought a gallon, though, ate half and promptly threw up.

And that is how fixed-odds betting terminals, Jamie Oliver and an ice cream stand in Bangkok Airport led me, via a bunch of calls to the show, to these two conclusions: The 'nanny state' is a phrase now used exclusively to describe mostly good and important attempts to prioritise citizen welfare over corporate greed; and 'classical liberal' now has nothing to do with Thomas Hobbes or Adam Smith. It's just a fancy phrase that kids who grew up without ever learning how to share use to describe themselves.

Chapter 7
THE AGE GAP

IF WE DO MANAGE to avoid an apocalyptic culture war, the biggest political battle on Britain's horizon will be based on age and money, rather than religion, ethnicity, gender or sexuality. There are two reasons why this is chronically under-reported. Firstly, it is creeping up on us incrementally and inevitably casts friends and cherished family members rather than any convenient 'other' as the enemy. Secondly, you're not going to sell many newspapers to an ageing readership who are convinced that modernity has ruined their retirement, by telling them that they've actually ended up with a disproportionately large share of the nation's spoils and are now going to have to share with younger generations.

Born in 1972 (Generation X: 1966–1980) into ineffably middle-class comfort, I took three things for granted growing up: I would do as well as, or better, financially than my parents, I would go to university and I would get a mortgage and become a homeowner. These were not particularly bold presumptions and would be mostly borne out by the relevant statistics. For people born nine or more years after me (millennials: 1981–2000) the world is a completely different place. For the first time in living memory, it is likely (though not, of course, conclusively proven) that a majority of them will fail to match their parents' financial situations. Research in 2016 by the Resolution Foundation, for example, found that Britain's millennials earned £8,000 less during their twenties than the previous generation. Research published by the Institute for Fiscal Studies in February 2018 showed that the chances of a young adult on a middle income owning a home in the UK have more than halved in the past two decades. And while they are no less likely to attend university than their forebears, the IFS estimates that they will leave with an average £50,800 of debt. My generation routinely left with none.

My wife and I 'bought' our first flat when we got married in 2000. In fact, we borrowed the full purchase price from the bank, plus an extra £10,000 for furniture and suchlike, which we didn't ask for but happily accepted when offered. We were, at the time, earning decent but by no means spectacular wages at the *Daily Express*, and the flat we bought was on the edge of London's achingly fashionable Notting Hill. Today, I speak regularly to people with six-figure joint incomes who work in London but cannot afford to buy a home anywhere in the city. That's not quite true, of course. They can afford to buy a home. They are, in most cases, paying more in rent than they would be required to pay towards a mortgage. But because they cannot raise the hefty deposit now needed to secure a mortgage they are, in fact, 'buying' the home in which they live for their landlords. For all the talk of 'Polski Skleps', 'uncontrolled mass immigration' and changing demographics, this is surely the most profound alteration British society has undergone in the last 18 years.

Many people also on the 'winning' side of this generational divide are, however, remarkably reluctant to acknowledge it. I'm not sure why. Exchanges like the following are common-place whenever the subject of housing costs comes up on the programme.

Doris: My husband worked fifty hours or more a week in 1966 to get the money together for our first home. Young people today are too busy spending all their money on iPhones and holidays. If they knuckled down like we had to, they'd soon get themselves on the ladder.

James: Can you remember how much the house cost, Doris?

Doris: Yes I can. It was £3,500.

James: And how much was your husband earning?

Doris: Eighteen pounds and ten shillings a week.

James: So just under £950 a year. That puts him on just above the average income for that period and the house was just under. The big point is that the house cost about three and a half times what he earned in a year. It was the same for me and my wife 34 years later, though our first flat cost £180,000. And we didn't need a deposit. Today, the average house price is just shy of £230,000 and the average salary is about £27,000. In other words, the average house now costs about eight and a half times the average salary. It doesn't matter how hard they work, Doris, their experience is never going to be remotely comparable to the ones you and your husband and me and my wife enjoyed.

These figures are, of course, in the public domain and the calculations can be completed while the person on the other end of the phone is answering my last question. It is nevertheless remarkable how intractable people like Doris can be. Again, I'm not sure why. She's clearly neither stupid nor nasty, but there seems to be a psychological resistance to the idea that life is in any way harder for young people today than it was for her when she embarked upon married life.

Doris: Well, I still think they just need to work harder and stop moaning all the time.

James: OK, Doris. I'm going to do a bit of rounding up and down of the figures, but bear with me. What's a thousand times three and a half?

Doris: Three-and-a-half thousand.

James: Right. And that's how you could afford your first home. What's 30,000 times three and a half.

Doris: One-hundred-and-five thousand.

James: Blimey. I was just reaching for my calculator. Are you sure?

Doris: Yes.

James: And here's the thing. That's less than half of the national average house price these days. And we calculated it from a salary that's a couple of thousand more than the national average. If you were buying your first house under the conditions that young people face today, it would cost just over eight thousand pounds. Well over double what you actually paid.

Doris: Well, we would have bought a smaller house.

You can't win them all.

One of the most dispiriting aspects of conversations about house prices and their broader economic consequences is the speed with which the status quo appears to have changed. People from backgrounds similar to my own no longer presume that property ownership is their birthright. A few years ago, it was as if we were all operating under the collective presumption that things would somehow return to 'normal'. What's actually happened, I fear, is that our concept of 'normal' has changed. And it poses a really troubling question: what are people today actually working for?

My late father occasionally said that he didn't really become ambitious until I came along. He was probably mythologising the irresponsibility of his twenties somewhat – he was clearly a brilliant journalist – but I've recently come to understand what he meant. The difference between us hinges on what the late, great Christopher Hitchens and his friend Martin Amis used to call 'tramp angst'. It bears little or no relation to one's actual financial situation, but instead describes an often irrational fear of penury. Hitchens did not suffer from it, but the considerably wealthier Amis apparently does. My dad didn't suffer from it, but I do. For most of my early twenties, when I was trying and mostly failing to get a foot in the door of Fleet Street, I could lie awake at night for hours terrified of unspecified failure. My ambition was considerable but it was built more, I realise now, on dreams of security rather than status. I was conscious, certainly, that I wouldn't be enjoying any considerable inheritances from my parents, but I lived in mortal dread of being too poor to keep my head above water. The feeling persisted until relatively recently, though I am still a fully paid-up member of the section of society which can give itself conniptions by wondering how long we could survive if the pay cheques stopped tomorrow. For Dad, life was clearly much more of an adventure and only when the responsibilities of fatherhood settled on him did he determine to strike out in search of the financial security he felt it was his duty to provide. Within two years he was on the *Daily Telegraph*. For both of us, though, getting a mortgage provided the only realistic path toward the different kinds of security we craved. And for both of us, it was a relatively straightforward process. Today, even as moderately successful newspaper journalists, it would be beyond both of our means. The younger generation seem more resigned to this than angry. Presumably because they cannot see how anger would change anything and, increasingly, they have never known things to be markedly different. This, then is their 'normal'.

I wonder now whether our concept of financial security itself is changing. I ward off the tramp angst by working out what we'd be left with if those wheels ever did come off and thus reassuring myself that we'd survive. By far the most crucial element of this process involves downsizing to a smaller home and so being able to live mortgage free. The millennials who ring my show to explain, almost blithely, why they will never be able to buy a flat, despite earning considerably more than the average salary, seem to live in a manner best described as 'genteel hand-to-mouth'. They spend serious sums of money on leisure and consumption, not because they're profligate but because saving while renting is never going to meaningfully change their relationship with the property market. So, if I've understood what they tell me, they end up with little or no concept of the day after tomorrow. I find this staggering because in my own way, I have been as blind as Doris: if you grow up under one kind of 'normal' then it's very hard to accept that it bears no resemblance at all to the new one. Just as Doris can't quite see that she would be squarely on the losing side if her 1966 financial situation was transported to 2018, so I cannot quite understand how millennials can contemplate their financial situation without despairing. If they are not working in pursuit of some sort of ownership-based security then they are not working for the same reasons as Generation X. And if they are no longer aspiring to own the only sort of capital our social classes can realistically own – bricks and mortar – then what will become of their relationship with the capitalist system?

If you think I'm exaggerating the gravity of the situation, ask yourself these questions: what happens when all the people currently working and paying rent, stop working? Who will pay to keep a roof over their heads? There are several generations of potential pensioners coming down the tracks who will have nothing to show for their entire working lives. They will conceivably have paid enough rent to pay off two or three mortgages on behalf of their landlords, but will own precisely nothing. They will also, of course, need looking after. But with more and more homes being sold to subsidise the social care of their owners, another grisly spectre emerges: an awful lot of the millennials and younger people who see a far-off inheritance as their passport to property ownership will likely not inherit a bean. I appreciate that I'm often guilty of reaching for portentous comparisons with nineteenth-century society, but where else can the current situation lead but to an ever increasing concentration of wealth in an ever shrinking section of society, coupled with a concomitant catastrophic crisis in social care?

Of all the lessons I've learned from listening daily to people whose lives are very different from mine, this is the most arresting. And it moves from arresting to alarming whenever you posit the notion that there are only three ways to halt the runaway train of structural inequality: income tax, property tax and inheritance tax. Here, more than anywhere, the decades-long grooming of the British public by the right-wing media is profoundly insidious. The widespread and demonstrably false belief that foreigners, unemployed people, single mothers and sundry other scapegoats *du jour* are bleeding the country dry explains why so many of us are so resistant to any suggestion that we should pay more tax. It has also helped to create a sense that, while we worked very hard for our money, there are so many people getting theirs in return for doing nothing that it would be outrageous to tax us any further. David in Shepherd's Bush, who rang in to object to a Labour Party policy that would see the five percent of the workforce earning over £80,000 a year pay more tax, provides a helpful example of the mindset. Oddly enough, he was also a millennial.

David: I'm lucky enough to earn more than the £80,000 mark, as are most of my friends, and we work extremely hard to do that, right? So we do 15, 16 hours a day on weekdays and regularly do weekend work. I don't think that is reflective of the wider population.

James: I do often hear about teachers putting in 15 or 16-hour days, and when I'm hearing about paramedics working in circumstances you wouldn't wish on your worst enemy I just reject the conflation of hard work with high earnings. Of course you work hard, David, but you don't work by definition harder than people who earn less than you?

David: Not by definition, no.

James: Why aren't you a teacher? Presumably because you don't want to get paid the sort of money that teachers earn?

David: Look, I'm not saying that people who earn less work less hard.

James: You are, though. You really are.

David: Look, there are lots of people on low incomes who work extremely hard, right? Fact. But what I'm saying is, that everyone I know who earns over that amount works much harder than the average person. They worked very hard at university, they've worked their way up.

James: What field are you in, mate, if you don't mind me asking?

David: I'm a consultant, a management consultant. Now I'm not from privilege at all, OK? I work hard. The key question is what's fair, OK? So people who earn more should pay more, but I feel that we're getting to the point now where if taxes went up for me, it would feel distinctly unfair to me. Particularly as someone who lives in central London.

James: It's important to remember that you are able to exercise choice. You choose to put in the hours you do. You choose to live in central London. But I respect your choices. I really do. The question, though, isn't the one you phrase as being about fairness. The question is, if we accept that we need to raise more money from somewhere, where would you go for it? As a management consultant, presumably this is your area of expertise. When you go into a company to advise on how to increase their profitability, what do you advise them to do? Pursue people who've got money, or people who haven't?

David: The people who have the most should pay the most, but having a binary threshold at 80 grand makes me feel like I'm being penalised.

James: Well earn more then, David. Work harder. If you're unhappy about the amount of money you end up with at the end of the month, put in some more graft. That was precisely the message you rang in with, and I think we both realise now how hollow it sounds.

Did we? Frankly, I doubt it. But his generation's relationship with work is so profoundly different from previous ones. My dad, born in 1939 (Silent Generation: 1925–1945), arrived in the workplace with reasonable expectations of a job for life and a comfortable retirement. Like many if not most of his closest contemporaries, it didn't quite work out that way. Cost-cutting and shareholder-rewarding redundancies in the eighties and nineties inflicted irreversible change on the British workplace and the resultant fluctuations in income for workers of his generation impacted negatively on their retirement. But there were still enough of his peers staying the course to keep the notion of 'jobs for life' afloat when the baby boomers (1946–1964) started work. My generation (X) was, then, the first to recognise that getting on the bottom rung of the ladder was no longer any guarantee of staying on it at all, let alone scaling all the way to the top. This may explain why I fretted much more about the future than Dad ever did, though he may just have been much cooler than me.

Consider now the millennial condition of having my generation's employment insecurity without the ameliorating effect of attainable property ownership. The single, tangible thing that can reassure people of my age that we'd survive in the event of the tide going out – equity – is increasingly beyond the reach of generations behind me. Worse, their relationship with work is moving ever further from that of my dad's generation. It may seem an odd example, given that its most immediate impact was on London black cab drivers as opposed to avocado-guzzling hipsters, but the Uber experience highlights this perfectly.

The station where I ply my radio trade was, traditionally, a redoubt of clichéd cab drivers possessed of, shall we say, reactionary views. The stereotype of the loquacious Little Englander is, I've since discovered, actually very unfair but it is still chronically over-represented among the cabbies who call in to programmes like mine. To generalise wildly, they are uncomfortable with trade unions, immigration, Labour politicians and the European Union. The attitude to trade unions and support for the Conservative Party belies a mindset that throws their experiences at the hands of the so-called ride-hailing app into almost unbearably stark relief.

Like Beefeaters and Routemaster buses, it's easy to sentimentalise the London black cab. On rare childhood visits to the capital from Kidderminster, my little sister and I considered a ride on one of their pull-down seats to be as much of a ritual as popping into Harrods' toy department. So when drivers first started telling me how unhappy they were with Uber in 2014 I was keen not to let dewy-eyed sympathies cloud my judgment. The then Mayor of London, Boris Johnson, termed them Luddites, in an attempt to portray them as dinosaur-like opponents of progress. Horse and carriage drivers, went the argument, had objected similarly to the introduction of the petrol engine but common sense soon prevailed. But the more I talked to cab drivers, the more I realised that Uber, and other euphemistically termed 'disruptive technology companies' like Deliveroo, were actually at the vanguard of a rather serious assault on established commercial norms. In short, they seek to use massive investment to insert a middleman into business models which traditionally saw suppliers deal directly with customers. They use their deep pockets to set artificially low prices, until the market bows to their dominance and a near-monopoly is established. At this point, of course, the artificially low prices can be inflated and money which would once have passed unmolested from passenger to driver now sees a significant slice make its way into the pockets of shareholders and investors.

Along the way, the cabbies got royally shafted. As the Conservative politicians they mostly voted for accepted jobs with funds heavily invested in Uber (George Osborne) or hired advisers married to the company's head of PR (David Cameron), the 'ordinary working people' they professed to protect who had borrowed significant sums of money to join the trade after spending several years training found out that their exclusive right to 'ply for hire' had effectively been torn up and flushed down the toilet. I often wonder whether sympathy would have been more forthcoming if cabbies hadn't revelled in a reputation for having no sympathy for other people on the receiving end of right-wing sharp practice. I guess we'll never know, but Uber taught me two lessons. First, neo-liberal entrepreneurship in a post-industrial society will effectively involve identifying markets where normal people are earning a decent living in the hope of introducing technology that will see some of that money end up with neo-liberal entrepreneurs and their backers. Second, the risk of launching new businesses is being increasingly passed from the owners to their underpaid, overworked and widely exploited workforce. Because, although I feel genuinely and enduringly sorry for the London cab drivers, I feel a hell of a lot sorrier for the men and women driving under Uber's auspices. So sorry, in fact, that it's time for another bit of stark historic comparison.

I listened to a documentary on the radio last year that celebrated the life and work of the landscape gardener Capability Brown. One of his grandest projects, I learned, involved re-routing a river that ran through the grounds of a stately home. Hundreds of men from surrounding villages were employed for over a year to do the digging, and the results were judged a great success. At no point did the programme reveal what the hundreds of workers did before and after their river-digging exertions. Until relatively recently, my route to work in London took me past a small group of workers, mostly Eastern European, who congregated in Hammersmith early every morning in the hope of being hired – illegally – for a day's labour on one of the city's building sites. Again, I wanted to know what happened on the days – or weeks – when there wasn't any work for them. Such piecemeal employment used to be commonplace. Until unions came to exert a degree of influence over employers, it was normal for docks to be crowded with men hoping for, but by no means guaranteed, a fair day's wage for a fair day's work. When I look at companies like Uber and combine that view with what I'm learning about the millennial generation's relationship with work, I worry that we're heading back to a similar dynamic. With neither capital nor security on the horizon, they are working simply to survive. And while the trappings of technology and disposable income don't immediately support the idea that they are latter day river-diggers, their expectations are improbably but comparably low.

Wayne and Arthur are among the many listeners to my programme who I have come to know off air. Both are over ten years younger than me, and we first met when they came regularly to a comedy and current affairs show that I hosted at a variety of venues across London a few years ago. Initially we got along famously. One of them, Wayne in Basildon, has become both a friend and a regular contributor to the programme. The other, Arthur, subsequently became so vituperative towards me that I had to block him on Twitter. He works as a driver for a company that has a contract to deliver white goods for a major online and high street retailer.

Arthur and his partner – shifting fridges is a two man job – are not employed by the delivery company directly, but rather have a contract that requires them to undertake a certain amount of deliveries while paying the company for the use of their liveried van. You read that correctly. Arthur pays for the privilege of going to work in a van owned by a company that pays him no sick pay, holiday pay or pension contributions. While technically self-employed, he is obviously unable to work for any other company or employer except over and above his already full-time schedule. Indeed, if one of them is ill or otherwise indisposed and unable to source their own replacement, the rent for the van is still due. It means that, in twenty-first-century Britain, getting sick while holding down a relatively menial job sees the sick person not just lose their wage for the days they're off sick, but actually pay money to their employer (who's not technically their employer) for every day they're off the road. Even the river diggers got free shovels.

Arthur is, understandably, a very angry man and the target for his anger, with heartbreaking predictability, is immigration. He has persuaded himself that the only reason why he and his driver's mate have to endure such punitive and degrading working conditions is because some people who were born overseas also endure such punitive and degrading working conditions. Suggest to him that the real source of his impotence is a dearth of trade union power and collective bargaining and he will decry you as a 'leftie' before returning to the comforting banality of bogus immigrant-blaming. The company whose vans he pays to drive is a household name. I wonder how many of their customers know the terms and conditions inflicted upon the people delivering their washing machines.

Wayne's situation is similar. His work installing state-subsidised, environmental improvements in homes is more satisfying, but he is almost as exposed as Arthur to the vagaries of modern, largely invisible, employment practices. He doesn't get angry, though, because, he says, he understands the system even as it screws him. Being mixed-race, he's also less susceptible to the siren call of blaming the non-native 'other' for the self-serving behaviour of his bosses.

Their theoretical middle-class equivalent is also supremely relaxed about immigration but equally powerless in the face of her employer's untrammelled, politically-enhanced authority. For her first two years in her job, under legislation extended by David Cameron's government, she effectively has no rights in the workplace. Changes to employment tribunal rules mean that, even when she has recourse to the law (after two years on the payroll), the expense of the process is profoundly off-putting. She is increasingly likely to be on a short-term contract, with few or none of the benefits her parents' generation took for granted. And because the cost of renting and living in the cities where the work is concentrated is becoming prohibitively expensive, she is too fearful of losing the work she has to complain about her conditions. Arthur gets to blame immigrants; middle-class young professionals in similar situations, albeit office as opposed to van-based, are too well educated to fall for that, but instead fondly imagine that the Labour Party leader, Jeremy Corbyn, will somehow be able to deliver a brave new world.

So these are the new 'normals': bosses get to do more or less what they want, while workers either blame their plight on immigration or ignore it altogether because the cost of simply staying afloat has become so high. Neither constituency routinely expects to become a homeowner anymore and so the most fundamental aim of capitalism – security through property – is increasingly debased. The 'social capital' that might reasonably be expected to ensure their commitment to society's status quo – the health service, the welfare state, schools, public services, etc – seems increasingly under siege from precisely the same ideologies and commercial forces that are currently picking over the carcass of the black cab trade. The remaining protections that workers enjoy in modern Britain are indubitably in the sights of the right-wing politicians who talked of a 'bonfire of regulations' being a benefit of Brexit. And the news sources we might expect to be explaining and condemning these assaults upon the fabric of our future are once again silent, because their billionaire owners are set to make another killing from the new direction of traffic.

At the same time, if you suggest to people who've crossed the rat race's finish line that they should stump up more money than they were expecting to, they will greet you with understandable anger and refusal. Logic dictates that, in the short term at least, the only way to assuage the horrors of the generational divide detailed here would be to redistribute some wealth from the older haves to the younger have nots. Politically, though, this is close to impossible. Not only are the said haves unlikely to vote for a party promising to raise taxes on them and their estates, but, crucially, there is little or no support for the idea from those a little further down the food chain. The myth of the feckless unemployed ensures that people who should theoretically be in favour of tax rises for, say, the top 5 per cent of earners will, in fact, be opposed to them. This is partly because they think they might be in the 5 per cent one day, but mostly because they've been persuaded that 'their' tax is spent on 'foreign aid', EU membership and handouts for the lazy rather than old-age pensions, social housing, emergency services, social care, medical treatment and infrastructure.

If I'm right, and I hope I'm not, then we're heading towards an unprecedented reckoning. The younger sections of society, whose taxes will effectively subsidise the care of the ageing sections, are being required to work in circumstances and for wages vastly inferior to their predecessors', without being offered any permanent stake in that society. The older sections, meanwhile, cling to the illusion that the travails of their children and grandchildren are largely self-inflicted. If nothing else, it unravels the riddle of Jeremy Corbyn's popularity that still causes such bafflement in so many corners of the political and media establishment. He at least articulates the sense that things can't go on like this, that the Scylla and Charybdis of demographics and economics will crush us all, unless drastic action is taken. Beyond Brexit and the existential threat it poses to the Union, determining what that action will be is surely the issue that will define the coming decades of UK politics.

Chapter 8
TRUMP

IN 1990, A LITTLE-KNOWN American lawyer and author called Mike Godwin formulated a pithy little adage that would become known as 'Godwin's Law'. It states that: 'As an online discussion grows longer, the probability of a comparison involving Nazis or Hitler approaches.' It was, at the time, a neat distillation of the dangers of hyperbole when comparing modern political developments to Nazism. But times change. In August 2017, hundreds of white nationalists, Ku Klux Klansmen and neo-Nazis descended on Charlottesville, Virginia for a 'Unite the Right' rally that left one counter-protestor dead and 19 injured, after a man linked to white supremacist groups drove his car into the crowd. The American president, Donald Trump, commented afterwards that there had been 'very fine people, on both sides'. It prompted Godwin to tweet the following: 'By all means, compare these shitheads to Nazis. Again and again. I'm with you.'

Trump had, by then, been president for just eight months. It still beggars belief that he could so quickly have created an environment in which violent racists, anti-Semites and Nazi ideologues could march unashamedly – and unhooded – on American streets. Even more dispiritingly, those eight months had seen a slow ebbing away of the confidence people like me held in the idea that support for Trump would dissolve as the full extent of his political and personal depravity emerged. In retrospect, that confidence displayed a remarkable naivety. Trump himself had demonstrated a chilling understanding of the fact that his 'fans' would forgive him any moral or legal transgression when he was campaigning in January 2016 and said: 'I could stand in the middle of Fifth Avenue and shoot somebody and I wouldn't lose any voters.' He was clearly right. The only question now remaining is: why wouldn't he?

Like Mike Godwin, I used to think that comparing contemporary politics to past eras of fascism and Nazism was fanciful and, in most ways, spurious. I believed, I realise now, that holocausts and pogroms and the such like were undertaken by people who somehow belonged to a different species than my own. For all the books I've read by the likes of Primo Levi, George Orwell and Hannah Arendt, I never really recognised that the populations which allowed and undertook the vilest acts in human history were exactly the same as my own. This is an embarrassingly innocent position to see written down in black and white, especially as my job had left me more exposed than most to the rising tides of ancient hatreds and ignorant fury that would carry Trump all the way to the White House.

For all the talk at the time of 'economic insecurity' and the 'left behind', it is clear now that Trump appealed knowingly and deliberately to the notion that white people were deserving of a higher status in American society than any other group. In order to protect them from the painful process of thinking, he fed his following with fatuous and largely meaningless slogans which they could chant, cult-like, at rallies where he did things such as casually abuse a disabled journalist. When he used a TV interview to malign the parents of a fallen American soldier who happened to be Muslim*, it became impossible to pretend that anything other than weaponised racism was his stock-in-trade. Detailing here the extent of the deliberate dishonesty he employs and the absolute contempt in which he holds his supporters won't bring the rest of us any closer to understanding why they still cheer him. To fully understand Trump and his supporters you need, I think, to actually feel that your whole life is somehow somebody else's fault, that the status and respect you consider your due have somehow been denied you by gay people or black people or Mexicans or feminists.

It is palpable nonsense to the rest of us, but slogans like 'Lock Her Up' or 'Make America Great Again' are, as we also saw with Brexit, not just the fig leaves that lying demagogues like Trump give to their supporters to help them cover up the toxicity and absurdity of their own 'opinions'. They are also weapons to be wielded against the truth. For

---

* ABC News interview with George Stephanpoulous, 30/7/2016

example, by calling the actual news 'fake news', Trump manages to create an alternative reality where his lies are somehow not lies. I found it funny at the time, but the full extent of this con became clear just two days after Trump's inauguration. At a White House press briefing shortly after the ceremony, his then Press Secretary, Sean Spicer, described 'the largest audience ever to witness an inauguration, period, both in person and around the globe'. This was arrant nonsense, designed to placate his manchild boss and undermine bona fide reports of an embarrassingly low turnout, irrespective of the observable truth. But it wasn't the definitive proof that the 'fake news' narrative had already completely infected the relationship between the people and the facts. That came a little later, when the Counselor to the President, Kellyanne Conway, was interviewed on NBC's 'Meet The Press' on 22 January 2017. When asked by the presenter Chuck Todd to explain why Spicer would 'utter a provable falsehood', Conway baldly stated that Spicer was giving 'alternative facts'.

Hindsight is a wonderful thing, but while the real media was still poring over the election results looking to explain away the national aberration with facts and statistics (bless them), Kellyanne Conway was tacitly explaining that facts and statistics, in the conventional sense, were dead. This, remember, unfolded during the very first week of the administration and it demonstrates perfectly how introducing 'fake news' to the national vocabulary had already allowed Trump and his team to write their own reality. It's a crowded field, but my 'favourite' illustration of just how corrupting the combination of fatuous slogans and fake news rhetoric can be involves the man who was Trump's campaign manager when chanting 'Lock her up' with reference to Hillary Clinton first caught on. Clinton's 'crime' was to have used an email server that wasn't government-approved during her time as Barack Obama's Secretary of State. At the time of writing, Paul Manafort, who was running Trump's campaign and rigorously defended the chant, is himself locked up.

Take an angry person, tell them you feel their pain, give them a target for their anger and help them to switch off their brain. It's not complicated. Present them with a slogan to chant, without ever insisting that they explain what it means, and give them an utterly bogus, entirely self-serving version of events to support their delusional fury. So it is that Trump supporters can gloss effortlessly over the fact that one of their men has actually been locked up, while they continue to chant that Hillary Clinton should be – without being able to explain why. It's a depressing depiction of our fellow men and women but it's one which Trump understands implicitly. Treat people as stupid, hate-filled, gullible and mean while simultaneously helping them to blame all their problems on 'others' and they will love you for it. So much so, that you could shoot someone on Fifth Avenue and not lose a single vote.

The most compelling evidence yet that this infection has crossed the Atlantic came when it was reported that Trump's visit to the UK in July 2018 would feature an inflatable balloon depicting Trump as a giant, bright orange baby wearing a nappy. This outwardly innocuous, if childish, wheeze turned out to have all the ingredients of the hatemonger's favourite dish. Permission to fly the dirigible came, in part, from London's City Hall. British right-wing commentators, who had miraculously shed much of their professed disgust at Trump during the first 18 months of his presidency, seized upon the fact that this could be reported as the Mayor of London himself 'giving permission'. Why would they be so keen to do that? Because the Mayor of London, Sadiq Khan, is a Muslim. Why would they ignore the fact that the Metropolitan Police and air traffic control would also be required to give permission? Because the Mayor of London, Sadiq Khan, is a Muslim. And why would they completely ignore the fact that the decision was, in fact, taken by the relevant committee and did not seem to contradict any previous decisions? Because the Mayor of London, Sadiq Khan, is a Muslim.

I would like nothing more than to be wrong about this. But I'm not. The analysis impugns people I still consider colleagues and friends, but the infection runs so deep now that rank Islamophobia passes mostly unnoticed across the national media. I know I'm not wrong, because I get to harvest the results of the hate-mongering. Simple, quite funny, on-air questions like 'Why are you so cross about a balloon?' proved remarkably enraging. It is easy and important to laugh at them, but the people articulating this incoherent rage perfectly demonstrated how deep the infection of 'fake news', fatuous slogans and textbook hate-mongering can be. They are furious but don't really know why.

Jack, for example, rang me from Croydon in a state of near-apoplexy. About a balloon. There is no polite way of saying this – and I wonder increasingly whether the time for politeness in the face of such rank idiocy has anyway passed – but Jack has absolutely no idea how stupefied and deluded he has allowed himself to become. I'm a strong believer in hating the liars not the lied to, but the line is often blurred. Perhaps because, as we see here, their hatred often ends up being directed at me, for having the audacity to hold up a mirror and make them look into it. Trump gives them a catchphrase like 'fake news' but when its utter fraudulence is revealed to them, it's not Trump they get cross with. See also 'We want our country back'; 'Make America Great Again!' and 'Lock her up'.

James: Jack is in Croydon. Jack, why are you frightened of a balloon?

Jack: I ain't frightened of no balloon. I just think it's absolutely pathetic, and cowards like you aren't even going to turn up to this Donald Trump rally. You'll just sit there having a go at the radio.

James: Having a go at the radio? I'm *on* the radio.

Jack: Well you'll be shouting at your microphone and it will be coming out of my speakers.

James: That is generally how it works, yes.

Jack: I'm not really interested in your balloon. I'm going to get my drone out and fly it right into it.

James: What day?

Jack: I think it's a bit disgusting the way you have a go—

James: What day, Jack?

Jack: Sorry?

James: What day are you going to do it?

Jack: I don't know. Whatever the day is. Whenever the balloon goes up.

James: You don't know when it is?

Jack: No. I've got no idea.

James: So you're cross about a balloon going up on a day you don't know?

Jack: [Louder] I'm not cross!

James: Well, you sound quite cross, Jack.

Jack: I just think it's really pathetic.

James: Why? It's good to mock politicians, isn't it?

Jack: No. Not really.

James: Really? You don't think any politician should be mocked? What about mocking disabled journalists, where do you stand on that?

This, obviously, refers to a Republican Party rally in 2015 where Donald Trump mocked the disabled *New York Times* journalist, Serge Kovaleski. It is literally on tape and has been broadcast around the world countless times. Here is the *Washington Post*, in 2017, describing Trump's attempts to rewrite reality:

> *Trump has previously claimed he was not aware that the reporter, Serge Kovaleski of the* New York Times, *has an impairment that visibly affects the flexibility and movement of his arms. The billionaire says that, when he singled out Kovaleski for ridicule during a rally in South Carolina – 'You've got to see this guy,' he said, before jerking his arms spastically – he did not intend to call attention to Kovaleski's disability, arthrogryposis.*

And here's Jack, in Croydon, in 2018, showing that it worked.

Jack: Um. Where do you stand on fake news, James?

James: I'm passionately opposed to it. But you can't answer a question with a question.

Jack: I can't do it. I can't answer fake questions with fake answers. Sorry, mate.

James: It's not a fake question. How do you feel about the mocking of disabled journalists?

Jack: Fake news.

James: But we've seen the pictures, Jack.

Jack: Fake news.

James: So the pictures are fake?

Jack: Fake news.

James: OK. So how do we feel about the mocking of Gold Star families?

This refers to Khizr and Ghazala Khan, the Pakistani American parents of US Army Captain Humayun Khan, who was killed in the Iraq War in 2004. On 28 July 2016, they stood on stage at the final day of the Democratic Party Convention and took aim at several of Trump's policies, particularly his proposed ban on Muslim immigration.

Khizr asked of Trump: 'Have you ever been to Arlington Cemetery? Go look at the graves of brave patriots who died defending the United States of America. You will see all faiths, genders and ethnicities. You have sacrificed nothing and no one.'

Trump responded by suggesting erroneously that the speech had been written by Hillary Clinton's staff and insulting the parents, saying: 'If you look at his wife, she was standing there. She had nothing to say. She probably – maybe she wasn't allowed to have anything to say. You tell me.'

Jack: Gold Star families? Again, fake news.

James: You've seen it on your screen, Jack.

Jack: I've seen it on my screen, mate. Fake news.

James: How do you know the story about the balloon isn't fake news? Why have you chosen to believe this?

Jack: You're going nuts about it, and I know why.

James: Jack, I think it's funny. I'm not going nuts about it. I'm giggling. You're the one who's phoned me about a giant balloon. I don't think you've phoned me before. I just want to know why.

Jack: Because it's pathetic, James. I really cannot understand why you just keep attacking Donald Trump.

James: But we know why you can't understand that, Jack. It's because you describe all the facts that provide the basis for attacking Donald Trump as 'fake news'. So you can understand why! Come on, Jack, no one's that stupid. If you describe the evidence of your own eyes as 'fake news', then of course you can understand why people keep attacking him. It's not difficult to grasp that, if you describe facts as lies, then you've chosen not to understand. I can't really help you any more than that.

Jack: Give me some real facts and then we can talk about them.

James: I just have. He mocks disabled journalists, he boasts about sexually assaulting women, he's a multiple bankrupt ...

> **Jack:** Fake news.
>
> **James:** He mocked the parents of a Gold Star soldier.
>
> **Jack:** Fake news. Fake news.

It's still tempting to dismiss this position as exceptional, but it's anything but. The desperation to believe that Trump is not the man that recorded facts prove him to be frees his followers from reality. The rest of us can sit here tearing our hair out and wringing our hands, but Jack and pretty much every diehard Trump supporter I've encountered will just carry on blithely insisting that the emperor is most definitely not naked, even as his bare buttocks quiver on national television.

The question is, why? What is it that Trump, and to a lesser extent Brexit, offers people that is so supremely seductive they will voluntarily switch off their most basic critical faculties and deny observable reality? What is the snake oil, the Kool-Aid, the brain soap?

Brian in Portsmouth unwittingly provided an answer to these questions during the same balloon-based phone-in. He began, as most callers did that day, by demonstrating that, far from being exceptional, Jack's position is pretty much standard self-delusion for the people desperate to believe in Trump. The irony, of course, is that these are precisely the same people who've spent the last few years railing against the perceived hyper-sensitivity of 'snowflakes' and 'social justice warriors', attacking the notion of people wanting 'safe spaces' and insisting that 'you can't give offence, you can only take it.' Such is the strength of the cult, however, that its members are utterly blind to their own absurdity and hypocrisy. Brian thought he had a zinger of a question for people happy to see the balloon fly above Parliament Square in London.

> **Brian:** If your father-in-law were to come round your house for the very first time, do you think it would be common courtesy to put up a balloon up of him in the living room, paint him orange with a giant nappy on? How do you think that relationship would develop?

I should probably stress here that Brian is entirely serious. His words, written down, may appear comical but, to him, these points and questions are both intelligent and important. Worse, the speed with which they fall apart invariably feeds into the victimhood status these people have been inculcated to bemoan. I haven't yet worked out how to defuse this sorry situation. Brian is about to embarrass himself on national radio but not, as he will see it, because he has fallen for the lies of devious and divisive people, or allowed his irrational fears and anger to cloud his judgment. It's because I am 'better educated' than him or 'living in a bubble' or 'out of touch with ordinary people'. And there are plenty of people in the mainstream media happy to inflate this ludicrous conceit. The *Sun* put it best when they described me as 'the epitome of a smug, sanctimonious, condescending, obsessively politically-correct, champagne-socialist public schoolboy.'

If you can't play the ball, as all bullies know, you try to play the man. Again, the ad hominems, like the slogans and the chants, become fig leaves with which the faithful can hide their abject failure to understand or think about anything. It's why they are often so surprised by what happens when they're asked, politely, to actually explain the words that have just come out of their own mouths. On Facebook, in the newspaper comments sections, in internet forums and even on other phone-in shows, these bovine arguments go unchallenged so poor saps like Brian are entirely unequipped for even the most cursory scrutiny.

Back to him and my fictional father-in-law.

James: Does he publicly abuse disabled people?

Brian: James, you've got to respect the office.

James: But you're talking about my father-in-law. Does he publicly abuse disabled people?

Brian: I don't believe that happened, and that was in the campaign before he became President of the United States.

James: So did it not happen, or did it happen in the campaign before he became president? Because you just said both.

Brian: The incident you're referring to happened during the campaign.

James: So did this man abuse disabled people before he became my father-in-law?

Brian: I've got ... I've got no idea.

James: But it's your analogy!

Brian: But James, won't you answer the question? Would you put a balloon up? Do you think that's common courtesy?

James: Yes, Brian if he routinely abuses disabled people and grabs women by the vagina, then I would probably seek to ...

Brian: And how is that helping things in the climate of Brexit?

James: If you don't stand up to it, you encourage it.

Brian: What's it going to do for the economy though, James?

James: Brian, I know you thought you had some brilliant points when you rang in, but every time I deal with one you try and move on to another one.

Brian: What's it going to do for the economy?

James: What's what going to do for the economy?

Brian: Isolating the United States of America.

James: Mate, he's just launched a trade war against his closest allies.

[Pause. Brian laughs a little manically.]

Brian: OK, James. You don't seem to have an answer, so I'm quite happy to leave it there.

James: I don't have an answer to what, Brian?

Brian: Well you don't … you're not really answering … I mean do you, do you …

James: I've answered all your questions. 'What would you do if your father-in-law came round?' Would I put up a balloon mocking my father-in-law if he was a serial sex pest? If he boasted about grabbing women by the vagina? If he routinely abused and mocked disabled people in public? If he took the mickey out of the families of a dead American – or indeed British – soldier? If he endorsed and implemented a policy that separated babies from their parents and threw them in cages in latter-day concentration camps. I don't think I would put up a balloon, Brian—

Brian: You wouldn't!

James: Because I don't think I'd let him into my house, however much I loved his daughter. And I'm fairly confident that I wouldn't have fallen in love with her if she was comfortable with that kind of behaviour, even from her own father.

Brian: And you can say categorically that Donald Trump is guilty of all those things, can you?

James: Yes, I've seen it. I've heard the tape of him boasting about being a sex offender; I've seen him mocking disabled people on television and I've read the order that his Attorney General Jeff Sessions introduced on 6 April 2018. But do you know what the really interesting thing is, Brian?

Brian: Go on.

James: You could see it all too, if you opened your eyes.

Brian doesn't want to open his eyes. He wants the big orange man-baby to sell him a baseball cap and give him a cuddle and tell him everything's going to be alright. I'm not expecting any prizes for pointing out, repeatedly, that authoritarian fraudsters only prosper when a population has been persuaded that an invisible enemy army exists. So it is that every terror attack by an Islamist madman can be proof that 1.6 billion Muslims wish 'us' harm. So it is that every sex offence committed by someone a bit foreign-looking can be proof that every migrant in the country is a rapist. But Brian said something else that day that didn't really sink in until after the show. He said: 'You're on the same side as Sadiq Khan and Brendan Cox,' and, unwittingly, blew the lid off his own previously impenetrable delusion.

As mentioned, Sadiq Khan is the Mayor of London. He is also a Muslim. His election to the mayoralty of, forgive me, the finest city in the world has proved to be kryptonite to racists on both sides of the Atlantic. It's not hard to understand why. He gives the lie to three of the alt-right/neo-fascist Islamophobe's most effective lies: 'ordinary working people' are sick of Muslims, the problem is 'their' failure to integrate and 'they' all wish us harm. It wasn't immediately clear why his election stuck so stubbornly in the craw of the Breitbart/ Infowars/Trump axis, but it is now. You can't get much more integrated into British society than getting yourself elected as mayor of the UK capital; a Muslim isn't going to be elected mayor by a population that is 'sick' of Muslims and a politician trying to tackle everything from air quality to knife crime can hardly be portrayed as harmful. They try to do so, of course, but the idea that Khan is somehow encouraging street crime in order to usher in sharia law as a solution is, currently, too outlandish for all but the most committed of crackpots.

For the record, I have been unimpressed by some aspects of Khan's mayoralty and encouraged by others. He is a tricky interviewee because, as a former lawyer, he is particularly adept at dodging questions. I remain to be persuaded that a tragic spike in knife crime has more to do with his leadership than the huge police cuts visited upon the city by central government and hope to see more substantive action on the 'affordable housing' front. I'm not going to speculate about what Brian in Peterborough meant when he spoke of me being 'on the same side' as Khan, in the context of a conversation about a racist, misogynistic American politician who fallaciously blames immigrants, Muslims and people with foreign-sounding names for all his country's woes. You can, though.

Brendan Cox is the widower of the murdered British MP, Jo Cox. A week before the Brexit referendum and hours after Nigel Farage unveiled his 'Breaking Point' poster, grimly reminiscent of Joseph Goebbels' Nazi propaganda, Jo was shot by a white supremacist terrorist. So perhaps Brian was suggesting that being 'on the same side' as Brendan Cox meant being opposed to murderous white supremacists? Or perhaps he was referring to the fact that Cox stepped down from two charities he founded in his wife's memory after being publicly accused of sexual harassment and a 2015 assault while in a previous job, saying: 'While I do not accept the allegations contained in the 2015 complaint to the police in Cambridge, Massachusetts, I do acknowledge and understand that during my time at Save the Children I made mistakes.'

When this happened, in February 2018, my Twitter feed exploded with alt-right and Trump-supporting Brits convinced that, because I had welcomed Cox into the studio several times and endorsed his condemnations of far-right rhetoric and terrorism, his public shaming would somehow reflect badly on me. This, I hope, is what Brian in Peterborough was alluding to, and it provides a fascinating insight into the cultish mindset. Because those aligned with the neo-fascists are so committed to their 'side' of the perceived battle or 'culture war', they will overlook every transgression of their leaders and comrades. The other side must, they believe, be similarly committed to their own cause. So when someone like Brendan Cox – who achieved public prominence only after his wife was murdered in broad daylight by a far-right terrorist – transgresses, people like me will somehow make excuses because we are 'on the same side'. Perhaps Brian in Peterborough was depicting my side as the one intractably opposed to white supremacist murderers while his, presumably, supports them. Or perhaps, just as wrong-headed but nowhere near as scary, he simply thought that my 'side' would excuse wrongdoing of its members in the same way that he had found himself on national radio defending the honour of a man who has previously been accused of rape by one his own ex-wives. We'll never know.

And that, I think, is where we are now. Truth has been completely and deliberately debased by the most powerful man on the planet, a man whose entire life has been spent persuading poorer people to enrich him further by acting against their own interests. But Trump, for me, is more symptom than disease. His political success was made possible by creating an environment of fear and loathing into which he could insert himself as saviour and protector. Historians of the future will marvel at how the malign influence of 'news' sources like Breitbart, run by Trump's *consigliere* Steve Bannon, could have gone unchecked for so long. They will point out that nobody really objected when Trump decried facts as 'fake news' but anointed the Infowars loon, Alex Jones, as reliable even after Jones had described the Sandy Hook school massacre as a hoax and the parents of dead children as hoaxers. They will struggle to understand how 'liberal' (by which I simply mean people who don't subscribe to a hierarchy of humanity) commentators and politicians completely failed to foresee his success. And they will point, baffled, to all the instances that should have set off much louder alarms, but didn't.

When you speak regularly to people persuaded that the evidence of their own eyes and ears is 'fake news' while the demonstrable lies of their leader are somehow the truth, you realise that the answers are, again, not political but psychological. The *Washington Post*'s valiant attempt to record every demonstrable lie Trump tells in office stood at 4,229 after 558 days in office. The people who ignore or pretend not to believe this do so because they enjoy being frightened and thrive on anger. It is, in many cases, all they have. In almost all cases, it is the only thing that can rescue them from the realisation that their unhappiness and grievances probably owe more to their political heroes, their own past votes and actions than the existence of a Muslim mayor, a Polish plasterer or a Mexican housemaid.

And yet, at the risk of doubling down on my own naivety, I still don't think they are bad people. Imagine, for a moment, what an undiluted diet of news portraying Muslims as terrorists, Mexicans as rapists, black people as criminals and feminists as metaphorical castrators would do to you. Imagine curating your own media to provide constant and unchallenged endorsements of your own warped world view. And imagine how effectively any occasional fears that you've been gulled or brainwashed or manipulated would fare under the entirely accurate observation that 'the actual President says it's all true'.

So while some of the snake oil is indubitably being served up by some profoundly evil people, it is still not fair to tar all their customers with the same brush. If you can see people 'on the other side' as genuinely believing that all the usual minorities and scapegoats really do wish them harm and really are responsible for their low wages or poor housing or hospital waiting lists, you should be able to see them in a more charitable light. And I think we need to see them in a more charitable light if we are going to unpick the mental contortions that can lead a chap like Brian in Peterborough to be passionately convinced that monsters do exist and that he is on the 'other side' of history to a man whose wife was murdered by a white supremacist or a mayor whose only offence is being Muslim. Or, for that matter, a radio presenter who deals daily with the dangerous delusions of the Brians and the Jacks but still, however horrible their rhetoric and however personal their abuse, refuses to believe that things have to be like this. And one who intends to keep shining lights under all their beds.

EPILOGUE

TRYING TO WRITE A BOOK about contemporary society poses one rather obvious challenge: society has a habit of changing before you've finished writing. For example, when I looked at ways in which the trans-Atlantic calamities described in the book might be remedied, Paul Dacre ceasing to edit the *Daily Mail* in the UK and the removal of Infowars from social media platforms in America were near the top of my wish list. In the last few days both of those prospects have become reality, but there is still some way to go.

From the House of Commons to Hungary, it's clear that some modern politicians in pursuit of power are more than prepared to flirt with the feelings and prejudices that brought Europe to her knees in the last century. In an ideal world, journalists would be in the vanguard of the resistance. But we're not. Whether through the insatiable appetites of a 24-hour news cycle or because decades of comparative peace has bred complacency about the prospect of it ending, much of the media appears dedicated to argument and concocted conflict as opposed to fact and evidence-based reasoning. Even the prospect of a return to the days when 'fake news' had a literal meaning and no 'facts' were 'alternative' brings little comfort, when you consider that the largely objective American media has been effectively hobbled by the marriage of Donald Trump and Fox News. When the liars have the loudest voices, the tellers of truth need to find new ways to be heard.

The assault upon objectivity began, for me, with climate change. On one side of the question of whether humans were contributing to global warming sat almost all of the world's relevant scientists. On the other were a few attention-seeking journalists and the former chancellor, Nigel Lawson. Nevertheless, any TV or radio debate on the issue in recent years has afforded equal time and weight to both 'sides'. It would, of course, be wrong to completely outlaw crackpots and quacks, but we seem to have reached a point where, if the moon landings happened today, producers would feel compelled to give people claiming the footage was filmed in an aircraft hangar in Kentucky the same prominence in discussions as Neil Armstrong.

Soon after climate change opened the door to this peculiar 'false equivalence', vaccinating children against measles, mumps and rubella became a debate due to the intervention of a single, soon-discredited doctor and a raft of self-appointed campaigners. In August 2018, Italy's recently installed 'populist' government removed mandatory vaccination for children, while in Britain crowds of ignoramuses have taken to gathering at the gates of hospitals in protest because they believe they know better than the doctors inside how chronically ill children with incredibly complicated conditions should be treated.

For me, this path leads inexorably to Brexit and an almost surreal exercise in obfuscation and dissembling that has seen prominent Leave campaigners allowed to completely contradict statements they made during the campaign more or less unchallenged by interviewers. I don't know whether there is either the time or the political will to stop Britain's exit from the EU now, but as we draw ever closer to the prospect of a so-called 'no deal', it's clear that major news outlets have learned nothing from the debacle of the referendum campaign. We are still putting bloviating blowhards in studios opposite World Trade Organisation experts and international trade negotiators. On the one side, detailed, depressing and frequently alarming accounts based on learned knowledge and experience; on the other a pantomimic insistence that everything will be fine if we all only 'believe' more. I have, for example, learned more about the customs union from van driver called Ciaran who calls me regularly than Digby Jones, Jacob Rees-Mogg and Iain Duncan Smith will collectively ever know.

One of the other central themes of this book, the reintroduction of inflammatory racism into the mainstream, makes contemplating what will happen next a profoundly unsettling experience. How confident can we really be that, if the sunny Brexit uplands of Boris Johnson's imagination turn out not to exist, his admirers will lay the blame at his blundering feet? A reported meeting with Steve Bannon, followed quickly by an ugly attack on veiled Muslim women, perhaps provide a clue as to the direction in which he would seek to take the country. If the media does not pull its socks up sharpish, the blame for a disastrous Brexit will be directed at everyone who warned that Brexit was likely to be disastrous. Already, a clamour is growing around the idea that arrogant inadequates like Liam Fox and David Davis could somehow have performed much more effectively, if only 'Remainers' had stopped pointing out how little they seemed to know or understand about the tasks they had set themselves.

In America, the best hope for democracy and truth is that Donald Trump ends up in jail, or at least in deposed disgrace. But even that could present more problems than it solves. The sheer absurdity of what some of his core supporters have been persuaded to believe – the latest nonsense, QAnon, contends that he is secretly leading an international fight against an enormous and omnipotent network of paedophiles – makes me worry at what might follow if the Constitution proves up to the task of removing the sort of president it was designed to resist.

Back in Britain, the rise of the mysteriously funded think tank continues apace. The TaxPayers' Alliance, for example, or the Institute of Economic Affairs have the appearance of venerable institutions and are treated as such by everyone from the BBC down, but how often are they asked about their financial support or encouraged to explain precisely whose bidding they are doing? If you cannot account completely for who is paying your wages, you should have no place arguing for political change in a British TV or radio studio, and you should certainly never see your 'research' reported as news.

The problem, of course, is what the programme makers will do if they are denied this inexhaustible supply of self-appointed experts prepared to argue with, well, science. Or the phalanx of shady outfits publishing papers that provide a nice 'news' line by suggesting that everyone should pay the same rate of income tax or that all unemployed people would find work if their benefits were completely stopped. We need a complete reversal of the idea that every argument has two equal sides, that every question is debatable and that every story needs to be 'balanced'.

If you're interviewing someone who has completely contradicted himself on, say, Brexit then don't let him punt his latest rubbish until you have held him to account for the last lot. Play the tapes, read the quotes, insist that he explain whether he was being deliberately misleading or simply mistaken. If a guest is booked on one issue then justify her presence in the debate by highlighting previous mistakes she has made in the same field. Create an environment in which politicians will be too frightened to drawl out yet another deceitful soundbite secure in the knowledge that it will be forgotten by teatime and, for the love of God, tell them that if they refuse to answer simple and straightforward questions about their own past pronouncements, they will never be allowed to darken the studio door again.

If the government won't put up an official spokesperson to defend or explain a policy or a problem, leave it undefended and unexplained. Tell listeners and viewers that nobody in actual power was prepared to talk to voters about this crucial issue. Don't fob voters off with another talking head or let an attention-seeking backbencher take five minutes of flak, in return for a pat on the back from Central Office and a knighthood 20 years down the line. And, when a minister does put his head above the parapet, don't let him answer a question you haven't asked. Don't let him insult us all by going off on a clock-watching tangent and then complain that he isn't being allowed to speak when you interrupt him. Interrupt him again. And again. And keep interrupting him until he either answers the question he's been asked or admits that he can't. If that seems too uncomfortable a challenge, stop socialising with these people. Stop being friends with them outside the studio. Our job is to hold them to account, not to keep them sweet in the hope of a flattering quote on the cover of our next book.

Make it crystal clear that, for example, Jeremy Corbyn could have a prime interview slot on any programme in the country any time he wanted. Drown out the democracy-defying hogwash that he shouldn't talk to the 'mainstream media' because it's so biased against him, by making it clear that he can have all the time in the world to prove his fitness to govern after he has been asked a few questions that potential Labour voters want answers to. And if that's too much of a challenge for him, ask how someone who can't navigate an interview is going to run a country.

And send journalists out of the cities and the south-east, to the parts that left comfortable London reeling when the Brexit result came in. Not as a special feature or an investigation, but as an integral, essential part of the daily news. Describe realities. Don't let the concerns of people who feel dispossessed and ignored be co-opted by racist rabble-rousers on the one hand or conspiratorial 'anti-MSM' cowards on the other. Tell their stories. Don't hold cosy little debates about their lives and concerns, experience them first hand and report them back to those of us who don't know nearly enough about what's happening on our watch.

Because it is our watch. There isn't anybody else.

AFTERWORD

I *still* don't know what they think they won. Brexit was supposed to have been delivered on 29 March 2019. It has now, unless the House of Commons bends to the Prime Minister's will at the fourth, fifth or sixth time of asking, been postponed until October at least. EU negotiators had managed to secure the agreement of 27 separate, sovereign governments to the 'Withdrawal Agreement' drawn up with their UK counterparts. And yet Theresa May failed repeatedly to secure the support of one government: her own. In a succession of Parliamentary votes on the putative legislation, many Conservative 'Brexiters' voted both for and against it. Few managed to do so quite as shamelessly as Jacob Rees-Mogg, chair of the so-called European Research Group of Brexit hardliners, who explained on the 27 March: 'I won't abandon the DUP because I think they are the guardians of the union of the United Kingdom'. Two whole days later, he abandoned the DUP and voted for the Withdrawal Agreement he had previously described as 'slavery'.

His turnaround is a useful illustration of how impossible it was to make meaningful predictions about the process at the end of 2018. Until that point, my two simple aphorisms, *'Leaving the EU will be like trying to get the eggs out of a baked cake'* and *'The minute you write it down, it falls apart'* had held up remarkably well. In order to deliver the abolition of freedom of movement that Prime Minister Theresa May seems to consider a genuine prize, she drew up the 'red lines' of UK withdrawal from both the Customs Union and the Single Market. But as soon as these 'red lines' met a central purpose of the Good Friday Agreement – economic and political equality on both sides of the border in Ireland – almost everybody versed in Irish politics concluded that the two things simply could not coexist.

If 'Brexiters' were to have their much-vaunted freedom to negotiate new trade agreements unilaterally, then Northern Ireland would have to forego membership of the Customs Union and thereby leave the regulatory frameworks of the European Union, while the Republic of Ireland remained within them. But if the island of Ireland were to now host two separate customs arrangements then not only would you need checks at the border between the two, but it would become impossible to sustain complete economic equality on both sides. Existing technology has not yet provided a solution to border checks without introducing infrastructure at the border, so, in an episode of political surrealism worthy of the great Flann O'Brien, Brexiters insisted that 'alternative arrangements' could somehow deliver what existing technology could not. The fact that nobody could explain what these 'alternative arrangements' might be did nothing to prevent them from being talked up by all of the usual suspects, and eventually enshrined in the so-called 'Malthouse Compromise'. The EU insisted throughout that there was no prospect of accepting such flimsy proposals but Brexiters persisted in promoting them, apparently believing that if they said the same thing, only louder, then the foreigners would finally acquiesce.

The 'backstop' at the heart of the Withdrawal Agreement insisted, very simply, that the whole island would remain in the same Customs Union until a solution to the problem explained above was delivered by the UK. Brexiters now found themselves in the astonishing position of arguing that not only was such a solution simple to deliver (although they couldn't tell us what it might look like) but also that it was unacceptable to have any requirement to stay in the Customs Union until this (very simple but apparently unexplainable) solution was delivered. This merits repetition, not least because its base absurdity seemed to elude much of the British media. The same people who insisted that the solution was simple responded furiously to the EU's insistence that things in Ireland would stay the same until that supposedly simple solution was in place. Again, TV and radio studios were stuffed with politicians insisting the EU would eventually buckle under the weight of our intransigence, remove the backstop or specify a date when Ireland could become host to two separate customs arrangements without any actual customs checks, thereby honouring the terms of the Good Friday Agreement. Are you still with me at the back?

It is important to explain here – not least because it too seems to have eluded much of the British media and all of the ERG – that the EU wanted to confine the retention of the Customs Union to the island of Ireland. They contended, quite reasonably, that the incompatibility of May's 'red lines' with the Good Friday Agreement was a distinctly Irish problem and so demanded a distinctly Irish solution. But the DUP, upon whom Theresa May ordinarily relies for her Parliamentary majority, would not wear this. While conveniently overlooking issues like abortion legislation, they are publicly adamant that there can be no divergence in law between the UK mainland and Northern Ireland. So it was that the EU agreed to extend the Customs Union to the whole of the United Kingdom in order to not only help Theresa May hold together her Parliamentary majority, but also to ease the passage of the Withdrawal Agreement through the House. It was, in other words, a considerable concession and was rightly described as such in the Irish media. For their UK counterparts, alas, this was barely understood and hardly ever explained.

Throughout this national psychodrama, the EU insisted repeatedly that there was no prospect whatsoever of reopening the Withdrawal Agreement (as did Theresa May for a few weeks at the end of 2018). Meanwhile, a new breed of Brexiters

– arguably even less well-informed than the ones who enjoyed the most prominence during the referendum campaign – insisted that they would do exactly that. Andrew Bridgen, a backbencher whose popularity with producers was not dented one jot by his admission on Radio Ulster that he believed he was entitled to an Irish passport by dint of being British, repeatedly argued that the 'EU will blink and offer us better terms'. Furthermore, his fellow ERG member, Mark Francois, seemed to suggest that the EU's clear and consistent position could be ignored because his late father had fought in the Second World War. Of course, the EU did not 'blink'; the Withdrawal Agreement was not reopened. Taking back that proverbial control culminated in the British Prime Minister waiting outside a room, while leaders of the 27 countries remaining in the EU argued within about how much time they would grant her to try, yet again, to get her Withdrawal Agreement through her own Parliament.

With all this self-inflicted turmoil dominating the news agenda, it became easy to lose track of how comprehensively the promises made during the referendum campaign had fallen apart. Whether it was Boris Johnson's airy visions of 'sunlit uplands' where we could 'have our cake and eat it', David Davis's insistence that 'there will be no downside to Brexit, only a considerable upside', or Michael Gove's claim that 'the day after we vote to leave we hold all the cards and we can choose the path we want', it is hard to see how they could have been proved more wrong. But no matter. The division inflicted upon our population by the lies and exaggerations of the Leave campaign had become so entrenched that most Leave voters remained loyal to the men who had so egregiously misled them. In a development that took even my battered sensibilities by surprise, callers to my radio show started claiming that they knew that things were going to go so badly *because the Remain campaign had told them so.*

So it was that while much of 'Project Fear' was quietly rebranded as 'Project Fact', many Leave voters were reduced to claiming that they had, in fact, known all along that they were voting for national self-harm and economic damage. This heart-breaking scenario provides perhaps the best illustration of how Brexit support had become faith-based and almost entirely divorced from the facts. I have spoken to many people who now insist that they voted to Leave precisely because they knew that Remain campaigners were right and that their own side was wrong. The notion that the economic damage we were inflicting on ourselves would be 'short term' was a fig leaf of sorts. But it fell off when prominent Brexiters like Jacob Rees-Mogg and the former CBI chief Lord Digby Jones started stating that it might take, respectively, fifty or even a hundred years to improve. Even more worryingly, these people now talk of a Brexit reversal as somehow betraying the 'will of the people', without once mentioning that it was the 'will' of 'people' to believe things that have turned out not to be true.

And that is where we are now: isolated, divided and confused. It seems unlikely that unity and reconciliation will be advanced by the insistence of men like Boris Johnson and Nigel Farage that it is not their fault that the Brexits they promised have failed to materialise. Sadly, recent history suggests that their attempts to blame anyone but themselves will find a willing audience among voters now insisting that they never believed in any of the promised Brexits anyway. Similarly, we advocates of a Second Referendum – or a so-called People's Vote – struggle to convey our sincere concern for misled Leave voters without sounding patronising or condescending. After all, however we dice it, we are also calling them gullible. Throw in the fact that diehard Leavers are now, with some success, attempting to frame any criticism of the Brexit promises they made as a denigration of the people who fell for them, and you are left with the unsettling suspicion that things are going to get worse before they get better.

It was, on a personal note, intensely gratifying to stand on the stage at the People's Vote rally in Parliament Square on 23 March and see a handful of placards displaying my latest attempt at a slogan of rapprochement: 'Contempt for the conmen. Compassion for the conned.' But it was just a moment. Shortly afterwards I realised that, despite the title of this book, I have absolutely no idea what will happen next. It was a strangely liberating realisation, but also a terrifying one.

15 April 2019

A NOTE ON THE TEXT

I HAVE TRIED WHEREVER possible to reproduce on-air conversations verbatim, and every effort has been made to accurately reflect the original conversations as they happened. However, I've changed names and a few other details where appropriate because, while many of the dialogues reproduced herein have already reached a wider audience via the internet, it seemed a bit fairer, as nobody ever rang a radio show expecting to end up in a book!

ACKNOWLEDGEMENTS

I WASN'T SURE I had a book in me until Jamie Joseph and Joel Rickett invited me to Penguin Random House for tea and biscuits in late 2017. By the end of that meeting, we had the germ of this idea and I had, in Jamie, a publisher who has proved as patient as he is perspicacious. His characteristically wise decision to ask Liz Marvin to edit the book paid particular dividends. I am enormously grateful to them both.

They wouldn't have invited me to tea at all if the curious combination of contemporary politics and developing social media technology hadn't conspired to make clips from my LBC radio show go remarkably – and still rather unbelievably – 'viral'. And that wouldn't have happened if my friend and colleague, Adrian Sherling, didn't possess such a keen eye and ear for what might prove popular. He really is, to adapt a very flattering Buzzfeed headline about me, the man who made the man who made radio go viral.

ACKNOWLEDGEMENTS

I wouldn't have had the opportunity to enjoy this whole process if numerous bosses earlier in my career hadn't demonstrated such faith in my supposed skills. Rob Hooker took a punt on a stand-in presenter who had only got in touch with the station because he had a tax bill to pay and very little work in the diary. Subsequently, Steve Kyte, Scott Solder, Mark Flanagan and David Lloyd resisted the temptation to replace me on air with someone people had actually heard of. When Ashley Tabor founded Global Radio and took over LBC it marked the beginning of a remarkable transformation. He, Stephen Miron and, most of all, Richard Park made me feel like we should be playing in the Premier League after years in the lower divisions. When James Rea was put in charge of the station, that dream began to become true and it has been a particular pleasure to share in his success.

I have been lucky, in my 14 (!) years on the radio to have worked with a handful of brilliant producers, all of whom became good friends. Maxie Allen, Lucy Fergusson, Michael Keohan and Caroline Allen have all played important parts in the show's success while indulging my – for them – frustrating enthusiasm for doing no forward planning, booking very few guests and not deciding what we're going to talk about on air until the very last minute. Remarkably, after so long in the job, I'm still enjoying it more than ever and that is in no small part due to my current team, Beth Woodbridge, Ivan Laskov and Ava Evans. A special mention here for Jones the

Engineer, or Clive as most people know him. The calm advice and rubbish jokes he has whispered into my headphones for most of those 14 years have been invaluable. Too many assistant producers to mention here have also helped enormously by working to implement my brief that the phone-in genre is at its best when quality of callers is put far above quantity. It hasn't always been easy for them; on many occasions I've berated them for not putting anyone through to the studio despite the switchboard being full and they've had to remind me that they are enacting my own instructions.

John Chittenden, LBC's Senior Publicity Manager, has held my hand with kindness and intelligence as I've made the rather strange journey from interviewer to interviewee. Counting bona fide broadcasting legends Steve Allen, Nick Ferrari and Clive Bull among my colleagues for the duration of my radio career has allowed me to learn from masters of the art. We certainly don't agree with each other about everything, but there is an intimacy and immediacy about the best 'personality' broadcasters that I have been privileged to witness first hand on a daily basis.

A special word here for John Gilbert, ostensibly my lawyer but in reality so much more: counsellor, stalwart support and valued friend. Thanks also to my friend, Andy Taylor, Rochdale's finest and one of the soundest men I know. And to Luke de Lacey, for providing much needed distraction from work and the news by playing countless games of FIFA against me on the Playstation.

ACKNOWLEDGEMENTS

Finally, and most importantly, the women in my life. My mum, Joan, and sister, Charlotte, who along with my late dad, Jim, helped me hone whatever debating skills I have over the dinner table. Especially Charlotte, with whom I did little but argue between 1982 and 1995. And thank you to my wife Lucy McDonald who, in the words of Jack Nicholson's character in *As Good As It Gets*, makes me want to be a better man, and to my magnificent daughters Elizabeth and Sophia. Without them, I would have had this book finished in a fraction of the time!